W0259810

THE ISIS PERIL

ADVANCE PRAISE FOR THE BOOK

'In recent years, increasing militant activity through the South Asian region has strengthened, rather than diminished, the premise that there is a strong presence of the Islamic State within the subcontinent, an area already deeply fraught with religious tension and political undercurrents. In this valuable book, Kabir Taneja articulates these concerns and challenges with an inside-view and painstaking research. His insights and analysis do a great deal to expand our understanding of this global threat closer home, and indeed to open our eyes to the footprints already in the sand. This is a chilling account; essential reading for anyone interested in understanding the risks.'—S. Hussain Zaidi, bestselling author and journalist

'In his book, *The ISIS Peril*, Kabir Taneja takes us through the rise of the Islamic State in Iraq and Syria to its inevitable spread outward to the point of threatening with a presence in parts of India. He traces the rise of ISIS from the aftermath of the US attack on Iraq in 2003, the online indoctrination of some Indians, while others joined the movement for the caliphate, the sophisticated online campaigns and the appearance of ISIS flags in Kashmir, which was an inevitable outcome of yet another failed military intervention by the US. Taneja highlights the psychology of South Asian jihadists from the Holey Bakery attack of 2016 in Bangladesh to the Easter weekend 2019 in Sri Lanka, underlining the threat to South Asia. In the process, Taneja deconstructs its strengths, exposes the movement's fault lines, and throughout maintains an intelligent, engaging, and analytical narrative on the geopolitical consequences of ignoring the ISIS peril. In India, we seem to have largely underplayed the looming threat as we remain complacent. This well-researched and lucidly written book, one hopes, would help us understand the nature of the threat where even a military defeat of the ISIS will not be enough to remove the long-term threat.'—Vikram Sood, former head, Research and Analysis Wing (R&AW)

'In studies of the terror that ISIS and other pan-Islamist terror organizations unleash, it is easy to miss the basic contradiction: that while ISIS claims to represent the cause of Islam, the largest numbers of its victims belong to the Muslim faith, and that several parts of the world where Islam's followers reside like South Asia haven't actually seen ISIS and Al-Qaeda gain much traction. Kabir Taneja's book is a refreshing read, among the first of its kind, looking clinically and with evidence at ISIS's desire to spread to the region, particularly India, and the real truth of its limited success thus far.'—Suhasini Haidar, national editor and diplomatic affairs editor, *The Hindu*

THE ISIS PERIL

THE WORLD'S MOST FEARED TERROR GROUP AND ITS SHADOW ON SOUTH ASIA

KABIR TANEJA

PENGUIN
VIKING
An imprint of Penguin Random House

VIKING

USA | Canada | UK | Ireland | Australia
New Zealand | India | South Africa | China | Singapore

Viking is part of the Penguin Random House group of companies
whose addresses can be found at global.penguinrandomhouse.com

Published by Penguin Random House India Pvt. Ltd
4th Floor, Capital Tower 1, MG Road,
Gurugram 122 002, Haryana, India

First published in Viking by Penguin Random House India 2019

10 9 8 7 6 5 4 3 2

The views and opinions expressed in this book are the author's own and the facts are as reported by him which have been verified to the extent possible, and the publishers are not in any way liable for the same.

Those referred to as 'accused' have been so named and recorded in the NIA files as accused in criminal cases, many of which are still pending conclusion. The author has used NIA files for his references and is making no personal observation or conclusion on the guilt of any individual, which is for the courts to decide.

ISBN 9780670091560

Typeset in Bembo Std by Manipal Technologies Limited, Manipal
Printed at Replika Press Pvt. Ltd, India

www.penguin.co.in

To my parents,
Narendra Taneja and Rasham Taneja

‘War was always here. Before man was, war waited for him. The ultimate trade waiting for its ultimate practitioner.’

Cormac McCarthy, *Blood Meridian* (1985)

Contents

Introduction

In 2013, as a reporter with a small Delhi-based weekly newspaper covering foreign affairs, I got interested in a small part of the Middle East that was going through a conflict between certain groups—a conflict that had started to get a lot of traction on social media. At the time, the fallout, if you will, of the Arab Spring in the region was hogging most of the Western media space, with drastic political changes in the offing in the extended region. Given the 'tyranny of distance' prevalent in the Indian media or simply its reluctance to spend on actual reporting, wanting to look into what was happening in the aftermath of the Arab Spring, specifically in Iraq and Syria, was not a very sellable idea. But oddly, it was this small newspaper that could afford giving space to what would become the biggest story in foreign policy, national and international security, and terrorism in the world over the next few years with the rise of the terror group ISIS and its brand of terror that could be beamed into our living rooms rent-free.

'It is not a big threat to India; not sure why you're trying to portray it as one here,' a senior Indian official told me as

I tried to report on Indian preparedness, specifically when it came to the internet. However, it quickly became glaringly obvious how effectively the internet was being used to sell a bizarre concoction of Islamist ideologies and almost a make-believe land with the promise of purity and piousness for the Muslim world, away from the 'ills' of Western and other civilizations.

The Russian campaign in Syria against ISIS found a lot of takers during this period. As I reported on the rise of ISIS in the region, former and serving diplomats backed, and at times marvelled at, Moscow's air campaign against ISIS in Syria. This sentiment was inspired in part by a post-Cold War hangover and a disdain for a United States of America (USA) under Donald Trump.

In 2017, as the dust around the Arab Spring settled, powers that were wishing for the demise of Syrian President Bashar al-Assad's regime started to reflect that this outcome was getting unlikelier day by day. In New Delhi, the ambassador of Syria, Dr Riad Kamel Abbas, who gained his higher education from India, addressed a gathering of thinkers, journalists, writers and students interested in foreign policy to apprise them of the situation back home. This was not an easy time to do this, with reports of chemical weapons being used by the Assad regime on his own people doing the rounds and creating an international outcry against an already embattled presidency. This address by Dr Abbas could have been a spectacle, with strict and pointed questions, but instead many of the former, older diplomats ended up sympathizing with Syria, backing the regime mostly against US misadventures in the region and the general approach Washington has had in the Middle East over the decades. Sensing the room as being in their favour, the Syrian delegation ended up fielding mostly light questions. The scene was perplexing, to say the least.

'They're bastards,' one former Indian diplomat, who has extensively dealt with the Middle East, told me about how he saw the Americans and their influence in the region. Nonetheless, both the USA and Russia were fighting ISIS to defeat the terror group, and simultaneously working in their own geopolitical interests in the region, with the former looking to cement its hold and the latter looking to uproot US hegemony.

This was still the period when ISIS and its sympathizers were mostly running amok in Iraq and Syria, and its effects were being felt in Europe, which was tackling a giant wave of migrants fleeing war in the region. South Asia was always expected to be a big target due to its large Muslim population. For the threat ISIS posed was the product it was selling, and not necessarily the group itself—a peril further amplified by the security agencies' undermining of its online presence and the dangers it posed. ISIS marketing its ideology well was the threat, and security agencies, used to seeing the defeat of terror as only being possible from behind the trigger of a gun, took their own time to finally come to a realization that the terror group had changed the DNA of Islamist jihad itself. Terror was no more the same as the kind the security agencies had been trained to defeat.

Hierarchies, organizations, chiefs, and leaders—all these traditional aspects of terrorism were demolished by ISIS. The era of Do-It-Yourself terror had started, and in South Asia, a small nation was going to be the most unexpected venue of one of the biggest pro-ISIS attacks in the world.

Easter weekend, April 2019, the island nation of Sri Lanka was getting ready to celebrate the long weekend. 'It's the island mentality,' people from the small country in the Indian Ocean, ironically shaped like a water drop, would often say when asked how they are so laid-back.

It was not always so on this tropical island. The year 2009 saw the end of one of the most gruesome and bloody civil wars known to mankind, as the Sri Lankan state defeated the Tamil terror group known as the Liberation Tigers of Tamil Eelam (LTTE). The Tamil group, fighting a secessionist battle for an independent Tamil state in Sri Lanka's north, is still considered by many as the most fearsome and well-organized terror group to have ever existed, even more so than Al Qaeda (AQ), and now, ISIS.

On 21 May 1991, while on a campaign trip to Sriperumbudur in Madras (now known as Chennai), in the state of Tamil Nadu, members of the LTTE walked into a political rally held by then Indian Prime Minister Rajiv Gandhi. During this interaction, an LTTE group member, wearing suicide vests, detonated their payloads in close proximity of Gandhi, killing him. This was a mere two months after India had ended its involvement in the Sri Lankan civil war through the deployment of the Indian Peace Keeping Force (IPKF), aimed at dismantling the LTTE.

The island nation had been under tremendous duress until some sort of peace prevailed over the past ten years. Sri Lanka, a melting pot of cultural and ethnic diversity, has had its fair share of struggles with conflict between various communities. Nonetheless, the wakes in its social fabric were contained to hyper-regional issues and not aligned with any larger, global effort by radical organizations to make Sri Lanka a part of their dossier. Even during the LTTE's time, the terror and ensuing war was for a local, ethnic cause, and not a larger religious narrative.

All of this changed on 21 April 2019 when multiple bombings targeting churches and hotels were conducted on the island. Eight suicide bombers—two of them sons of a local millionaire—took part in the act, which ended up killing more than 250 people. The terror strike was blamed on a local Islamist outfit, the National Thowheed Jamath (NTJ). However, two days after the attack, what some feared came true. The so-called Islamic State (IS), or Islamic State of Iraq and Syria (ISIS, also known as ISIL or Daesh, in Arabic) claimed responsibility for the strikes. Over the next few hours, as the casualty numbers rose, other bombs that had been found were defused and raids conducted, ISIS released pictures and videos of the Sri Lankan attackers, calling them fighters of the Islamic State.

The NTJ was so far a largely unknown organization with some sketchy information available prior to the strikes. Believed to be a splinter group of the Sri Lanka Thowheed Jamath (SLTJ), another Islamist group known for attacking and defacing Buddhist statues in a small part of central Sri Lanka.[1] Either way, both NTJ and SLTJ exist within a very hyperlocal ecosystem, and the latter's apparent secretary, one Abdul Razik, was involved in activities inciting hatred against Buddhists. Razik later issued an apology for his behaviour.[2]

Perhaps this apology offers a quick look into what we will see further in this book, explaining how and why ISIS grew at such a fast pace, what were the characteristics that appealed to so many Muslims, educated and uneducated alike, who fell for the story sold by the group. It could be said that when Razik's apologized, other members of the SLTJ realized that their leaders were just not radical enough, causing them to go their separate ways. Such a rift within a group such as the SLTJ would not be new; in fact, this kind of division within an organization was one of the principal factors behind the creation of the Islamic State itself, as disagreements over ideology erupted amidst Al Qaeda hierarchies.

South Asia, despite its significant political and social complexities, had until this moment largely escaped from regular major attacks conducted by ISIS. However, today, the Sri Lankan bombings stand as the largest ISIS or pro-ISIS act of terror since the official establishment of the terror group in 2014. And it happened in Sri Lanka, a country no one was expecting to be in the crosshairs of the group. This blind spot is perhaps what led to the success of this strike for ISIS. Every country is fair game today for ISIS's 'Do-It-Yourself' style of terror, and in a world of globalized economics and politics, both facing significant stress themselves, a wedge in the idea of secular societies works in favour of the ideologies and world-view of these jihadists.

Over the past five years, the Islamic State and its caliphate—a geographic hold the terror group managed to establish over Iraq and Syria—has become the focal point of global security. In just a matter of a few years, ISIS not only challenged the sovereignty of states in the Middle East and as far as Libya, but also created multiple new layers of how we perceive traditional terrorism to occur.

Sri Lanka today has become ISIS's biggest success story, whether directly or by association, it hardly matters. But why Sri Lanka mattered to the Islamic State itself is perhaps the more important aspect of the attack to study. From its magnetic rise out of the Syrian civil war to its geographic demise in the dusty desert bowl of central Syria, the story of ISIS is not over yet. In fact, if anything, Sri Lanka acts as a primer to what may come in the future under what is today the biggest brand of Islamist jihad, the Islamic State. And to understand this further, we need to understand the history, roots, and ultimately the death of a proto-state, but not necessarily that of an organization.

To understand the Islamic State, we need to start from its end, in Baghouz, a parched piece of land in central Syria. The time that passed between this last fight and the Sri Lankan attacks was so important in the story of ISIS, that its leader Abu Bakr al-Baghdadi, not seen since 2014, released a video on 29 April 2019 restamping his authority and almost relaunching ISIS like he had done five years before.[3]

End of the Beginning

In a sparsely populated piece of land in the middle of the desert in the south-central region of Syria, the relatively stable Arab state and its leader President Assad were being challenged by a cocktail of rebels and militias. Soon, the country was in flux, with intense fighting taking place in almost every corner, affecting millions of people and killing thousands.

In this dry region known as Deir Ezzor, not too far from the Iraqi border, a conglomerate company, made up of Indian and Chinese money and local Syrian partners, operated an oil investment, which was to become the first major crisis New Delhi would have to attend to as Syria lost control of its state. While India was theoretically far from the fallout of the Syrian crisis, in 2013, New Delhi was faced with its first challenge as Islamist groups slowly took away territories from under the control of Assad and developed miniature proto-states, which they governed themselves. Here, like any other such conflict, the control over natural resources was going to be critical for any group's survival. And it being the Middle East, oil was almost always just around the corner.

Amidst these political pushbacks by the people of the region against despotic regimes ruling over them for decades on end, the rise of the Islamic State in Iraq and Syria (ISIS), a radical Islamist group that no one could have guessed would become how we know it today, was getting stronger day by day. The situation had taken a radical turn, with some even raising existential questions over the territorial integrity of the region itself and as to how long these borders as we know of them today would survive.

ISIS had taken to using regional oil reserves, predominantly in Syria, to finance its acts of violence and the expansion of its agendas. According to estimates, the Islamic State until recently was earning up to $1 million per day by selling oil produced from makeshift refineries on the black market. Incidentally, the Kurdish Peshmerga were also relying on smuggled oil for funding. Eventually, the ability of ISIS to sell oil had diminished due to increased air strikes against them.

As the Syrian civil war intensified during 2012–13, Syrian diplomats made trips to India to try and garner support from the Indian government. They also tried to persuade other countries in the Britain, Russia, India, China, and South Africa (BRICS) association. Damascus looked to New Delhi for support in stalling any incoming large-scale military assistance for the now fractured opposition forum known as the Syrian National Coalition (SNC). On her visit to New Delhi, Assad's political advisor Dr Bouthaina Shaaban said that India was 'an important country for the political process on Syria.'

Meanwhile, in April 2013, India's ONGC Videsh Limited (OVL) lost control of its oil investments in Deir Ezzor, as the oil field where India was part of a conglomerate that had invested along with Beijing and others was overrun by rebel fighters, suspending all exploration and production activities in the area. Contrary to popular assumptions, India and China have in the past invested together in the Middle East and Africa without political or economic fallout.

Even though the loss of production from the fields was not especially significant to the partners (roughly 30,000 barrels per day), this situation offered both New Delhi and Beijing first-hand experience of losing energy assets abroad to non-state actors—a situation that may well become more common in the future as both economies are expected to remain some of the biggest buyers of Middle Eastern oil. The fight for access to Syria's modest oil fields by groups such as ISIS and others fuelled a war within the broader civil war, as provinces that hold these natural resources experienced overwhelming chaos with war lords, criminals, Islamists, corrupt officials and mercenaries, both foreign and domestic, trying to stake claim over the available black gold. These groups sold crude oil to middlemen who then passed on the supplies to various buyers, including those across the border in Turkey and even forces aligned with Assad's regime, who were as desperate for energy today as the rebel-held strongholds in Syria. The currency these smuggling operations brought in became critical to various groups operating within Syria.

The takeover of such natural resources in Deir Ezzor, Hasaka, Raqqa, and so on is a valuable example for countries such as India and China, who are looking to invest and build facilities in the region. The question of securing these facilities can clearly not be taken for granted simply on the back of a host country's influence and the investing country's political heft.

Even as the USA exerts a near hegemonic foreign presence in the region, the situation that has developed in Syria showcases the political complexities at play.

The loss of the Deir Ezzor fields represented a learning curve on asset protection abroad for Asian economies, which are already the world's biggest importers of oil and gas. The only thing to be done at that point of time by New Delhi was to abandon the field, and move its senior staff and management stationed there to oversee the business in Dubai.

The security of such installations, after this experience, would become a test for Asian governments as their thirst for fossil fuels will continue to increase over the next forty more years at least, which is critical for the celebrated Indian economic story to continue. Ideas were being floated by former Indian diplomats for a new forum consisting of major Asian powers such as India, China, Japan and South Korea to offer an alternative platform in the East for discussions between various power centres in the Middle East for long-term protection of such interests in the Middle East. This ideation, while it makes complete sense on paper, was geopolitically unattainable.

New Delhi, however, still tried and put its voice forward at the second Geneva negotiations on Syria in 2014. India's then foreign minister Salman Khurshid presented New Delhi's concerns over the ongoing crisis and its posture on what the resolution should look like. This showcased that New Delhi was worried about the potential fallout of the crisis and a larger spillover of disruption in the region.

'India has important stakes in the Syrian conflict. It shares deep historical and civilizational bonds with the wider West Asia and Gulf region. We have substantial interests in the fields of trade and investment, diaspora, remittances, energy and security. Any spillover from the Syrian conflict has the potential of impacting negatively on our larger interests,' Khurshid told the Geneva-II gathering.[1]

'We are encouraged that this Conference is a convergence of the positions of global and regional powers with India's own consistently stated position of supporting a comprehensive political settlement of the crisis. We have supported full implementation of Geneva Communiqué of 30 June 2012, which focuses on ceasefire and negotiations between all parties, leading to the formation of a transitional governing body and to be followed by democratically held elections. India believes that societies cannot be re-ordered from outside and that people in all countries have the right to choose their own destiny and decide their own future. In line with this, India supports an all-inclusive Syrian led process to chart out the future of Syria, its political structures and leadership. There can be no military solution to the crisis. India's stand on various resolutions in the Security Council and General Assembly has been in support of efforts to bring about an end to violence by all parties.'

The above lines can be viewed as a general umbrella framework on how New Delhi approached the Syrian civil war. By this time, ISIS was gaining steam, while the narrative of the crisis still largely resonated between two main blocks of thought, one coming from the West that the Assad regime must go and one from the East, namely Russia and Iran, that the regime must stay. The political vacuum which was being created by fighting over Assad was rapidly filled up by ISIS. Ultimately, personal agendas of states and influence blocks came in the way of a concerted effort to block terrorism.

However, perhaps no one could have imagined what the region had waiting for it. What would happen in Syria over the next three years would change the global approach towards terrorism and how and where it is fought. ISIS rose from these remote areas of Syria and Iraq, far away from the great capitals and cultural centres of Europe, the skyscrapers and economic might of the USA and the upcoming centres of all future growth in the Asian economies, and found ways to beam its propaganda into our drawing rooms, bedrooms, and smartphones used by children thousands of miles away, effectively and strategically. It became the biggest brand in terrorism, not just overtaking the likes of Al Qaeda, but making Osama bin Laden's alma mater insecure about its place as the world's most feared and hunted group. Achieving that is no mean feat.

ISIS changed the terror landscape worldwide, and they are not done yet.

The Origins

On the outskirts of Amman, the historical capital of Jordan nestled in the midst of the Middle East's cradle, home to some of the world's fiercest wars, exist the most loving men and women, and spectacular food. The region showcases the very best and the very worst of mankind—a paradox of human conditions, natural riches, and foreign interventions that has kept the contemporary populations hidden under the garb of conflict for much of the past five decades.

Jordan's barren landscape mixed with Amman's vibrant and active persona add a Hollywood-like backdrop to real life. The capital city hosts a clash between American capitalism and Islamic conservatism where everyone from CIA spies to top militia leaders can rub elbows with each other on the streets and in fancy restaurants, both knowingly and unknowingly. This quagmire of domestic and foreign politics in Jordan's neighbourhood makes the kingdom, and its stability, an in-demand commodity.

About 20 km from Amman's central districts rests the satellite town of Zarqa, where the mirage of a cosmopolitan Amman encounters the realities of social and economic disparity. Nestled in the area are largely shanties and semi-permanent structures. The tightly-packed locality is home to 500,000 people, making it the country's third largest population after the capital and the city of Irbid. Zarqa was to shoot to global fame as the hometown of one Abu Musab al-Zarqawi, born Ahmad Fadeel al-Nazal al-Khalayleh, a shy boy struggling in life after the passing of his father, only to find solace in violence, death, destruction and jihad. 'Zarqawi' is part of Khalayleh's lineage and identity, and this would be a trend of naming individuals that the world would witness when thousands of foreigners from around the world attempt to join the so-called 'Islamic State'.

The 2003 invasion of Iraq by the USA as a fallout of the September 11 terror attacks in New York in 2001, the largest terror strike in history against the Western world, was the starting point of the creation of the jihadist faction known today as the Islamic State of Iraq and Syria (some Westerners prefer to call it Daesh, its Arabic name, as a counter-narrative ploy). However, the perceived history of the militant organization is entangled, like many other Islamist groups and the conflicts surrounding them, in the sectarian divisions of Sunni Islam and Shia Islam, poverty, ideological heft and criminal routes emanating from the region's social structures.

The fall of Saddam Hussein's Ba'athist regime at the hand of the Western coalition, armed with wrong intelligence regarding the country's weapons of mass destruction (WMDs) programme, caused tremors in an already jolted society and polity. The vision of 'regime change' bringing peace and stability in the Middle East had been a long-standing fantasy of planners in Washington D.C., but has almost always led to nightmarish outcomes for the people of the region first, and later global security as well.

To date, in 2019, the USA after Iraq now looks towards Iran with similar fantasies of outcomes for entirely different reasons, but expectedly the same short-term victories will turn into long-term violent battles.

Osama bin Laden was at this moment the most wanted man in the world, and Al Qaeda was under severe pressure from US drone strikes and 'shock and awe' bombardment, which forced them to move inward from the frontlines of Afghanistan deep into the Tora Bora mountain ranges. However, this did not deter its affiliates around the world to pull back even as the central leadership was under duress for masterminding 9/11, and the likes of Al Qaeda in the Arabian Peninsula (AQAP) started to make their name in areas such as Yemen with the help of people such as Anwar al-Awlaki, a US citizen and a principal recruiter and motivator for the Al Qaeda brand. Awlaki, an engineer by training from Colorado State University, was perhaps one of the first to really realize the power of the internet and video-sharing platforms such as YouTube. His radical sermons, delivered in proper English, gave Al Qaeda a voice beyond the Middle East and the Arab world, and the Iraq and Afghanistan wars had provided the ideal canvas for painting these pictures to suburban American Muslims living the white picket-fence dream in the USA, or others in Europe who were, even after decades, struggling to integrate culturally and emotionally into society.

The dusty shanties of Zarqa were far from Iraq, but like it goes in the Middle East, any war usually has an effect on the entire region. However, Zarqawi's rise would be much more critical to the future course of Iraq than his native Jordan, despite the fact that his initial interest was to dethrone the Jordanian Hashemite kingdom. But he had much larger aims as well, those that would even have him confront Osama bin Laden.

The roots of the so-called Islamic State, the Salafist-jihadist organization which had managed to catapult itself to the status of the world's premier terror group over the past four years, can be traced to the late 1990s. ISIS founder and jihadist Zarqawi took to a life of crime and rebellion. He would eventually be targeted and radicalized by the teachings of his spiritual mentor, one Sheik Abdul Rahman. During its metamorphosis from being one of many regional Salafist groups in the Middle East to what can now be called the biggest and most influential terrorist organization in the world, ISIS has destroyed and recreated the narratives of Islamist terrorism previously held by the likes of Al Qaeda. While the now deceased Al Qaeda chief, Osama bin Laden, rallied funds and ideology to exclusively target the USA, the ideas that drove ISIS from its inception were more localized, targeting regional governments, and only later turning territorial in the hope of creating a caliphate.

The post-9/11 invasion of Iraq by the USA shot Zarqawi to overnight fame, and it remains a matter of debate whether referring to him as an 'international terrorist extraordinaire' was by design, realistic intelligence or a casual off-the-cuff remark by a staffer, which had not gone through due diligence of the intelligence apparatus. However, as of the current state of ISIS, which we will discuss soon, a mixture of all-of-the-above seems to have played a crucial role. It may be assumed that Zarqawi became a household name on 5 February 2003, when then US Secretary of State Colin Powell spoke at the United Nations Security Council (UNSC) to underscore the USA's case for the invasion of Iraq. 'I want to bring to your attention today the potentially much more sinister nexus between Iraq and the Al Qaeda terrorist network, a nexus that combines classic terrorist organizations and modern methods of murder. Iraq today harbours a deadly terrorist network headed by Abu Musab Zarqawi, an associate and collaborator of Osama bin Laden and his Al Qaeda lieutenants,' Powell declared.[1]

During Zarqawi's formative years, his country was going through a phase of great change, as conservatism, tradition and theology collided with largely US-led westernization of the Jordanian society. As it is in many such cases, Zarqa did not gain a lot from this. Zarqawi lost his father in 1984 when he was eighteen years old, and thereafter found himself going awry in life. Not long after, he was arrested and imprisoned on charges of drug possession and sexual assault. Zarqawi's time in prison was to be the tipping point. He was radicalized in prison, and after his release carried his indoctrination with him with a deep sense of purpose. After becoming a familiar face at the al-Hussein Ben Ali mosque near Zarqa, known to be popular with Islamist radicals, Zarqawi learned about the jihad against the Soviets in Afghanistan and was soon thereafter hired by the Afghan-Arab Bureau, an organization tasked with providing jihadists to the Islamist forces battling Moscow.

Zarqawi's journey as a violent extremist started from the basics, with a bunch of people that could only be seen as a small criminal gang at that point. One account narrates a story of one of Zarqawi's first plots in Jordan, where the aim was to blow up a bomb in a theatre showing adult films, a sign of Western cultural infiltration in his and his compatriots' eyes. One of Zarqawi's then associates was tasked with the job of targeting the screening using an Improvised Explosive Device (IED), which was low-yield but capable of causing damage and death in a small environment. However, the intended bomber upon entering the theatre got distracted by the film, and ended up missing his crude timer setup on the IED, setting off the explosion near his own leg.

Despite his enthusiasm, Zarqawi did not see battle in Afghanistan as the Soviets soon retreated. He arrived with his mother, Omm Sayel, in Peshawar, Pakistan, where the young son of Jordanian-Palestinian mujahid Sheikh Abdullah Azzam joyfully welcomed him. Here, he started showing his networking skills despite his reportedly coy nature. In Afghanistan, he also met Abu Muhammad al-Maqdisi (real name known to be Isam Muhammad Tahir al-Barqawi), a known Salafist cleric and fighter, and with his guidance understood both the political and military aspects of jihad against the Soviets. Not seeing any military action, Zarqawi along with Maqdisi returned to Jordan, where he started to build a terror network based on the spiritual guidance of Maqdisi. As a result of their initial ploys, which were mostly abject failures, both Zarqawi and Maqdisi were sent to fifteen years in prison for holding grenades in their possession and being part of a banned organization. Asked about the weapons during trial, Zarqawi replied that he had found them by the roadside; the judge was unable to see much humour in this reasoning, and sentenced him. However, getting imprisoned turned out to be a blessing for Zarqawi, as the seeds of radical Islam that he was already carrying were to be emboldened even further. He and Maqdisi set up a new organization called Jama'at al-Tawhid wa'al-Jihad (JTJ) in order to expand on their common agendas.

In prison, Zarqawi started to hone himself as an alpha-jihadist. He spent entire days memorizing the Quran; he gained weight and built himself up to physically look more authoritative and fearsome, and he succeeded in developing his repertoire and recruiting members. Soon, he surpassed Maqdisi in his clout and started to challenge the latter's spiritual authority, relying more on his own instincts than his adviser's spiritual and theological directions. After leaving prison, Zarqawi started his gradual ascent to become one of the most wanted men in Iraq; soon he would have a bounty of $25 million on his head.

It was in prison where Zarqawi made the decision to go to Afghanistan again to build a militia that could export his brand of jihad across the globe. In southern Afghanistan's Herat province, he founded the Jund al-Sham group. His camp managed to recruit a healthy number of fighters, numbering between 2,000 and 3,000 prior to the US invasion in October 2001. During this period of buildup in the year 2000, Zarqawi had also caught the attention of bin Laden, who later met him in Kandahar; by the few accounts available, he was received coldly. According to one account, Zarqawi told bin Laden that his jihad was not dedicated enough, suggesting that bin Laden and Al Qaeda were soft. Powell naming him the top draw in the US invasion of Iraq—whether a strategy or a mistake—had propelled Zarqawi's ego. From being a relative unknown, Zarqawi had become an entity willing to confront Al Qaeda head-on.

Bin Laden later invited Zarqawi to join Al Qaeda, despite his own strong reservations, in the hope of sorting out their differences and his own apprehensions regarding building a respectable presence in Iraq. However, Zarqawi was determined to concentrate more on regional operations, taking on corrupt Arab governments, and foremost, bringing down the Jordanian monarchy and installing an Islamist state. This plan clashed with bin Laden's larger view of concentrating on targeting the USA and Israel. Bin Laden's military commander, Saif Al-Adel, brokered a deal between them, making Zarqawi the leader of Al Qaeda in Iraq (AQI). Despite the impasse being broken,

Zarqawi, true to his defiant nature, refused to pay *bayat* (oath of allegiance) to bin Laden; leading to relations between the two plummeting even further. Zarqawi would only agree to the bayat in 2004 after months of negotiations, realizing that he needed to increase his legitimacy in Iraq, and at the time this was the only way to do it. The bayat provided him with his new title, 'Emir of Al Qaeda's Operations in the Land of Mesopotamia'.

Throughout this period beginning in 2004, Al Qaeda made multiple interventions to control Zarqawi and his extreme violent ways, fearing a loss of support from their base. For Zarqawi, who anyway thought that the likes of Al Qaeda and Taliban were not serious enough about jihad and the agenda for the global installation of sharia, such advice was not worth heeding. And he continued to defy any instructions from either bin Laden or his deputy Ayman al-Zawahiri, and orchestrated gruesome violence across Iraq while propagating the same across much of the Islamic world.

What is relevant here is that his founding of the Jama'at al-Tawhid wa'al-Jihad in late 2001 was the seed of what is called ISIS today. Under JTJ, Zarqawi started to train militants to conduct suicide bombings across the region, more specifically, in Iraq. The murder of United States Agency for International Development (USAID) officer Laurence Foley in 2002 by JTJ outside his home in Amman, Jordan, placed the group in the global limelight. By that time, Zarqawi also knew that a US invasion was imminent, and wanted to prepare on the ground with other militias. This plan included gaining the support of the powerful Iraqi Shia religious leader Muqtada al-Sadr, who had launched a military movement staffed by his supporters known as the Jaysh al-Mahdi.

Zarqawi's influence also attracted the interest of other major regional actors such as Al Qaeda. JTJ joined the Osama bin

Laden-led terror outfit in 2004, changing its name to Tanzim Qaidat al-Jihad fi Bilad al-Rafidayn, translated into English as 'Al Qaeda in Iraq'. During this period, AQI, whose top leadership was not always in tune with the thought process of bin Laden or his then deputy and now AQ chief Zawahiri, believed that fanning the flames of sectarian conflict within Iraqi society was the ideal strategy to gain a strong foothold in a post-Saddam Hussein era. This strategy of AQI was emboldened in May 2003, following then US President George W. Bush's announcement of an end to major military operations in the country, just days after the toppling of Hussein's statue in Baghdad's Firdos Square, symbolizing the end of his reign.

The evolution of AQI continued under the political vacuum created with the collapse of Hussein's order and the political infighting between the Shia and Sunni blocs. AQI, in the beginning, found support amongst the Sunnis, who backed the group in the hope that it would deter a takeover by a Shia-majority government in Baghdad. To maintain this public support, AQI engaged in frequent attacks against Shiite targets such as mosques and localities with majority Shia residents in order to fuel tensions and create an environment of distrust in local government formations. This, initially, brought in a broad base of support for AQI in Iraq, specifically amongst the minority Sunnis who feared a majority Shia-led Baghdad.

However, because of its increasingly violent streak which also killed Muslims, coupled with its more outward outlook of attacking US targets, AQI began losing ground base in Iraq, including within Al Qaeda. Zarqawi ignored advice from Zawahiri to build better ties with the Iraqi leadership. On the ground, AQI's relations with other Islamist factions deteriorated fast, and within Iraq its group of foreign fighters (from other countries such as Saudi Arabia, Lebanon, and Pakistan) were being seen as another foreign occupational force. What expedited the process of the Iraqi government trying to shut down AQI's operations were the group's bombings of three hotels in Amman, which killed sixty people, and the February 2006 bombing of the Shiite Al Askari Shrine in Samarra, 125 km north of Baghdad, which resulted in dozens of retaliatory strikes on Sunni targets within a period of 24 hours.[2]

To correct its course and build a broader support base, AQI joined the Majlis Shura al-Mujahidin (MSM), an umbrella jihadist organization consisting of around six Sunni insurgent groups dedicated to fighting the occupying US forces and stopping attempts towards a US-orchestrated transitional government, including pacification of the Sunni populations away from the jihadist narrative. The groups—Jaish al-Taifa al-Mansourah, Saraye Ansar al-Tawhid, Saraya al-Jihad al-Islami, Saraya al-Ghoraba, Kitaeb al-Ahwal, and Jaish Ahlul Sunna wa al-Jamma (note that the names of these groups could differ with different sources, as they changed often)—and AQI together planted the seeds of what would come to be known as a different jihadist entity all together, sans Zarqawi's leadership.

During this period of Sunni insurgent reorganization, dismantling and rearranging of leadership and structures, public support for the AQI was receding, as it was for the MSM—which by this time had fractured and was acting merely as a forum for bickering amongst its members. AQI, within the MSM, maintained control of the narrative and did not adhere to the idea of a centralized structure, and continued its practices of gruesome violence including beheadings and suicide bombings, causing great unease amongst the Sunni communities themselves.

These tactics employed by Zarqawi continued to bother Al Qaeda's top leadership, which had been encouraging Muslims across the world to travel to Iraq to fight the US invasion. AQI and the top Al Qaeda leadership, by around 2003, finally seemed to have found some common ground on how the former needs to operate in Iraq, and to what end. The August 2003 truck bombing of the UN headquarters in Baghdad was a critical point for Zarqawi, attacking what the bin Laden-Zawahiri leadership wanted, namely targets symbolizing US influence (albeit, indirectly). Following this, AQI moved to its original intended mandate of attacking local targets, among them, in governance and state structures, politicians, police, aid workers, NGO officials, and construction businesses.

On 7 June 2006, a US drone strike using 500-lb bombs hit a small house in the town of Baqubah, north of Baghdad, killing Zarqawi along with other jihadists. His undoing was, ironically, his spiritual guru himself, as intelligence officials tracked Rahman for weeks hoping that it would pinpoint Zarqawi's whereabouts. Abu Ayub al-Masri (also known as Abu Hamza al-Mujahir) was named as Zarqawi's successor to lead AQI, who took upon as his first job the recalibration of the organization by making it more 'Iraqi', to gather support lost on the ground due to Zarqawi's rigidness. Masri's takeover of the AQI was also a small victory for Al Qaeda who, as mentioned previously, had challenges in getting AQI to imbibe their own views rather than those of Zarqawi. However, Masri, a close confidant of Zawahiri, had little effect on the tempo of AQI—brutal killings continued, even got emboldened, as did the pacification of foreign fighters into the Sunni insurgencies. Zarqawi had left behind a new ideological and operational normal in the Islamist world in Iraq.

Taking over the command, Masri negotiated a new council of sorts, incorporating other regional insurgent groups under his ambit and declaring this new coalition as the Islamic State of Iraq (ISI) while keeping the AQI brand alive in an all-encompassing mentor role. Masri decided to place ISI's operations under a stoic man, a football fan born in the Iraqi city of Samarra, named Ibrahim Awwad Ibrahim al-Badri, known today as Abu Bakr al-Baghdadi. This would be the beginning of what is today known as the Islamic State.

The transformation of Al Qaeda in Iraq and the reaping of the ideological seeds Zarqawi had sown was just beginning, and no one, not even bin Laden, was in control of this Iraqi football fan from Samarra.

Welcome to Mosul

Mosul is Iraq's second largest city along with being one of the oldest in the world. The city, nestled on the banks of the mighty Tigris river that goes through its centre like a parade, has not only been the epicentre of ISIS with the setting up of its so-called Islamic State, but historically also been the very antithesis of the destruction and brutality that ISIS preaches and practises. Religions such as Christianity coexisted peacefully with Islam for generations in the city—a historical tradition that was, perhaps bizarrely, one of the legacies of the Hussein regime.

In July 2014, the history of Mosul changed overnight. Baghdad was in a political quagmire, which oddly had nothing to do with extremism or terrorism but with sectarian and tribal differences, which were the cause of much of the strife in the region. A quick glance at the map of the region will show you how Iraq is precariously situated between Saudi Arabia and Iran. Saudi Arabia, home to Mecca and Medina, Islam's holiest sites, is the flag-bearer and seat of Sunni Islam, which is in direct confrontation with the Shiite seat of power in Tehran.

One of the greatest questions around the rise of the Islamic State is how such a non-state insurgency group managed to become a militarily calibrated unit. During the period 2014–15, IS captured millions of square miles in both Iraq and Syria, serving a blow to the governments of then Iraqi Prime Minister Nouri al-Maliki, and Syrian President Assad, who continues to hold power.

There are many theories on the factors that not only gave birth to a terror group such as ISIS but allowed it to thrive in resources and territory. There is evidence in the hypothesis that the failures in Iraq revolving around the disbanding of the Iraqi Army and the subsequent sectarian and authoritarian Shiite government of Maliki offered a fertile environment for Sunni insurgents to recognize, organize and direct their agenda with ease both in the divided Iraqi-minority Sunni population and the thousands of fighters, officers and trained for battle Ba'athist regime generals who were now available, without a purpose.

After the US invasion toppled Saddam Hussein's sectarian Iraq and a by-the-stick implemented Ba'athist policy, 'Sunni disenfranchisement' gathered pace quickly. Being the minority, Sunnis in Iraq were worried over their own future in the country and the formulation of the new governance structures and their own representation within them. The victory of Maliki in 2006—much to the delight of the home of Shiite Islam, Iran—and his eight-year-long rule would provide the perfect canvas for AQI and other Sunni insurgencies to spread sectarian discord.

The starting point—or perhaps more aptly, the tipping point—was Operation Iraqi Freedom (OIF), the US war against Iraq to dismantle the regime of Saddam who, according to the

USA, was supporting and promoting terrorist activities and was in possession of WMDs. As part of OIF, a critical phase called ECLIPSE II (alternately known as PHASE IV, and named after ECPLISE I, which dealt with de-Nazification of post-World War II Germany) was going to go down in history as the biggest factor for the ease of militarization of not just AQI, but of various other intra-sectarian insurgencies as well.

The decision to disband the Iraqi Army, and make 4,00,000 troops and nearly 50,000 Ba'athist officials jobless overnight, had trouble written all over it. The Coalition Provisional Authority (CPA) was tasked with driving Iraq from the post-Saddam era to the progressive, democratic and inclusive vision of Washington D.C. and President George W. Bush. American diplomat Paul Bremer, who held solid credentials with his work previously in Afghanistan, and came under the supervision of Defense Secretary Donald Rumsfeld, led the CPA. With CPA, the USA orchestrated one of the most poorly judged political vacuums in the country, the aftermath of which the world continues to witness today. The USA disbanded the Iraqi Army with just a 'hand-wave gesture'.

During the period from 2003 to 2006, the USA held sole responsibility for the security of Iraq, and US troops were in every possible way seen as an occupying colonialist force, something Iraq is historically familiar with. Such optics were to gravely damage the US Iraqi project, far beyond the fallacy of the occupation to begin with, in the wake of Zarqawi being perceived as a mere proxy.

This vacuum split the now unemployed army veterans and Ba'athist officials amongst various insurgencies. With their trade being handling weapons, and killing—and no post-disbanding vocations or alternatives offered—the personnel found themselves more useful to the insurgencies against the Americans rather than sitting idly. AQI, and later ISIS, were to gain the most from this fallacy by Bremer.

The swift fall of Mosul in June 2014 and of Tikrit later the same month were treated as declarations by ISIS of both their capability and seriousness in acquiring a territorial governorate for the so-called caliphate. ISIS takeover of these regions of Iraq faced little resistance from Sunni minorities, despite their apprehensions as discussed earlier in this paper. Aided by an onslaught of media propaganda that showcased theatric beheadings of ISIS's opponents, the terror group faced a subdued challenge from Iraqi military and police forces. Both Mosul and Tikrit, under ISIS, got new governors, both former Ba'athists in the Saddam regime.

In the lead-up to this period, Maliki's policies in Iraq only inflamed the situation further. The militias fighting the likes of AQI began to come under heat, as Maliki moved to pacify the Sunni population. He cornered Shia cleric Sadr in Basra and forced him to surrender to the government, while disarming a host of other groups. However, Maliki's schizophrenic approach not only continued to diminish his own power in Iraq, but also cornered the USA on how to deal with the escalating situation. The Prime Minister started to replace Sunni and Kurdish leaders and officers in Iraqi governance with Shia ones while moving politically closer to Tehran, a foe of the USA, knowing well that the Bush administration had little option but to support him.

By 2014, the last year of Maliki's rule, the Sunnis were already in revolt against his government in Baghdad. As ISIS moved into Sunni-held areas of the country, they found themselves facing less resistance, starting with almost a welcome ceremony in Fallujah, as they took over the town in January of that year.

By this time, the seeds of ISIS ideology planted in Syria by Zarqawi and Baghdadi were growing. The idea of the caliphate was a territorial conquest of Iraq and Syria, and perhaps even beyond, if propaganda was to be believed. The 2011 revolt against Assad gave ISIS, dominant in Iraq, an opportunity to spread its wings and cement its presence. To emphasize its dominance and seriousness over territory, ISIS declared Raqqa, a city on the banks of the Euphrates river in Syria as its capital—a significant symbolic move considering that the insurgency originated from Iraq.

Syria, another sectarian theatre where the majority (Shias) were ruled by the minority Alawite government of the Assad family, almost simply landed in ISIS's lap. The uprising against the Assad family was an extension of the so-called 'Arab Spring', a string of protests over the ideas of justice and democracy in the smorgasbord of sectarian Middle East politics that had enamoured the global community. Like Iraq, Syria was also a sectarian experiment in the Middle East, with the majority of the population being Sunni, but having little representation in governance as the Assad family ruled the country for decades.

The Syrian theatre, like Iraq, gave many opportunities for various insurgencies to build on, including the Assad regime's opportunistic tactics to pitch these groups against each other and offer the narrative that Islamists launched the Arab Spring protests against his government. However, in Syria, it proved to be more complicated for ISIS as Al Qaeda and its now former affiliate, the Nusra Front, along with a host of other groups, some backed by the USA, created a complicated web of antagonists. The interventions of Russia and Iran to make sure the Assad government does not fall and ISIS does not control the Syrian borders with Central Asia caused further complications beyond the region.

Assad took over the reins of Syria from his father, Hafez al-Assad, chief of Syria's Ba'ath Party who launched a coup d'état in 1970, backed by the Soviet Union. This historical leeway made by Moscow in the 1970s still remains as its main access point to the region, and is seen as part of Russia's sphere of influence. The protection provided by Russian President Vladimir Putin to Assad over the past few years is Moscow looking after its only point of influence in a region where Western powers largely dominate the narrative, specifically with the Arab Gulf states. In a sense, the current situation in Syria over the triangulation between Damascus, Washington, and Moscow is a continuation of the rhetoric from the Cold War period. ISIS provided a solid reason for Russia to enter the battle on two main fronts—first, as mentioned earlier, to protect its only political and military entry point in the region and second, to genuinely make sure that ISIS does not try to either influence or relocate to Central Asia. As of 2016, reports suggest that nearly 2500 Russians were fighting in the ranks of ISIS. Unofficial numbers state a count of 8000 fighters and above.

Today, ISIS's brutality exhibited in Syria over the past three years is only part of the problem in the Syrian civil war. The Syrian Army is fighting ISIS, US-backed militias including the Kurds, and a cocktail of jihadist groups primarily fighting against the government but also amongst themselves. ISIS arguably had a more strenuous time in Syria trying to establish the caliphate than in Iraq, with groups such as the Nusra Front driving their own agenda, later even separately from Al Qaeda, for an

Islamist state, which by their design did not include the Assad government nor ISIS.

To put things further in perspective from Syria's point of view, in the battle for the so-called caliphate's capital in Raqqa, US-backed militias aided by US Special Forces and air support have made significant headway in pushing back against ISIS from the eastern regions of the country. However, like in many other parts of the conflict, as territory recedes from ISIS's hands, it does not represent an overall victory over ISIS.

With territorial losses, ISIS is leaving behind a huge political vacuum, similar to the one it had itself taken over during the period of 2014–15. However, the major difference on this occasion is that the vacuum has left behind even larger caches of weapons than ever before, and there is no one entity, including the Syrian government, that is ready to control these areas as a unit. Raqqa may yet become the first post-ISIS challenge for the US-led coalition, with a complex web of Shiite and Sunni militias, religious leaders, and legitimate regional actors such as the Kurds vying for territorial supremacy. However, the bigger threat will remain that a band-aid solution may be applied in a post-ISIS Syria, bartering the critical aspect of stability with short-term gains of military withdrawal and setting up puppet systems of governance. This, after all, is characteristic of the West's interventionist history in the region. Often, this trade-off between short-term objectives and enduring goals of economic and political prosperity gives rebirth to insurgencies, and ends up restarting the vicious cycle of violence, extremism and sectarianism.

While Iraq is a comparatively more straightforward war against ISIS, the involvement of Iran and Russia makes Syria a much more complicated theatre. While Iran-backed militias actively confront ISIS in Syria, they are also systematically creating space for their own armed factions as well as Hezbollah, and coming in direct conflict with not only anti-Assad forces, but Al Qaeda, the Kurds, US-backed militias, and various smaller Islamist groups vying for space vacated by ISIS.

Raqqa, at the time of this writing, was entering a phase where the eighth-century walls around the city had been breached by the Syrian Democratic Forces (SDF), an Arab coalition, and Kurdish fighters. Despite repeated marketing of the narrative of the loss of territory by ISIS as a 'victory' against the terrorist group, the battle for Raqqa has been, and is going to remain, a long-drawn one. While more than 50,000 civilians remain inside the city, acting as a shield between the warring parties, this jihadist status quo will perhaps continue for years to come. However, declaring victories and the 'liberation' of cities is also part of the war against ISIS narratives, specifically those raging around territorial conquests.

The battles waged in Iraq and Syria against ISIS are not going to be decided in the near future, as military achievements in containment differ from establishing a workable system to make sure ISIS or even other Islamist groups do not regain lost ground. In fact, scholars such as Charlie Winter, Senior Research Fellow at the International Centre for the Study of Radicalisation (ICSR) in London, have raised questions whether ISIS losing cities such as Mosul have been, in fact, false flag operations by the group. Winter argues that the ways of ISIS operations of inciting gruesome violence and committing grave atrocities against local populations such as rape and murder would challenge an insurgency's prominence within a given territory. Highlighting that the aim of ISIS to establish statehood had been a catastrophic failure, Winter puts forward a pertinent question: 'What if, more than anything else including territory, the group [ISIS] just wants permanence, to be the ideological hegemon of global jihadism? In this pursuit, the realization of ideological aspirations is far more important than the permanent administration of any piece of land, even if it comes at great material cost.'[1]

In all probability, ISIS will look into re-establishing itself as more of a guerilla movement than a statehood. The outcomes of such a downgrade towards ISIS's mandate as a group and perhaps more importantly, as a caliphate, are not yet quantifiable and existing research on this aspect of the insurgency is mostly grounded on conjecture at best. To understand the survivability prospects of ISIS, it is important to understand the group's operations as a state.

The Western mission name to defeat ISIS is called 'Inherent Resolve', directed by US military's Central Command (CENTCOM) based out of Tampa, Florida, with assistance from NATO allies. This mission has been running perpendicular with Russian air strikes, also against ISIS, in the same regions. The main target of both Washington D.C. and Moscow still is, at the the time of writing this, Baghdadi, who like a cat with nine lives, has been reported killed or gravely injured by both Russia and the Western coalition multiple times.

The USA–Russia kerfuffle in the Syrian theatre has been a series of ups and downs for both the powers, with its own set of repercussions and events that, in any other time frame of human history, would have had tumultuous consequences for global politics. However, during the phase from 2013–17, there was very little that was going to surprise the world politically. The initial battle against ISIS was a confused mix of a unilateral military approach by Vladimir Putin and a concentrated effort by the USA with its European allies that were on the cusp of facing a wave of refugees trying to escape ISIS's new state. The initial response was not easy for the international community itself, as the deconstruction of the threat that ISIS posed, despite their territorial claim, overlapped across the borders of two sovereign states in Iraq and Syria, with their own distinct political and social challenges that had no commonalities with each other.

Russia, however, took the bait and decided to blink first and launch military operations against ISIS. In December 2015, Russian Sukhoi 24 'Fencer' and Sukhoi 25 'Frogfoot' fighter-bombers targeted ISIS transport trucks smuggling oil near the Syria–Turkey border. While Syria is not known as one of the large producers of oil like some of its neighbours in the region, its output was enough to allow ISIS to earn nearly $2 million per day from smuggling oil and selling it. The main points of such smuggling were Raqqa and Tikrit in Iraq and Deir Ezzor region in Syria. Targeting the oil smuggling systems operated by ISIS was initially seen as a major way to disrupt their cash flows, with much of the 'trade' taking place via the Turkish city of Ceyhan. According to estimates, an ISIS produced barrel of oil was sold at around $17 per barrel, against a market price which was easily above $65 per barrel in 2015. This lowball pricing made ISIS-supplied crude popular in Ceyhan, and other landlocked oil providers such as Iraq's northern Kurdish autonomous region found its profits hit due to the smuggled supplies.

ISIS's approach towards Syrian oil fields was systematic and professional. It advertised positions for engineers to operate the fields, an approach it equated to being a state, and adhering to the rules of a nation-state with governance, economy and military taking precedence. Contrary to popular belief, ISIS was, in fact, robustly independent when it came to financing. Despite the narratives ranging from fact, propaganda and delusions of them being funded by a host of international donors, including the USA and Western alliances, the so-called Islamic State took over many existing state and private businesses which gave them a strong currency base to operate on. The initial boost came from the basic crime of plundering. After walking into Mosul and taking over the city, it is largely believed, without independent corroboration to date, ISIS gained access to banks in the city and walked away with nearly $400 million in loot, a figure that raised many concerns in the West over the prospects of such massive funding in the hands of one of the most violent terror organizations in the world.

The success of ISIS is not a chimera, in fact it is possible to factor it down to the basic issues and points that led to the rise of the so-called Islamic State, and Mosul itself provides most of the answers. The fact that parts of the population were receptive to ISIS had a lot to do with the sectarian fractures that existed in Iraq after the ouster of Saddam Hussein, and the inability of leaders such as former Iraqi Prime Minister Maliki to not only counter the growing drifts in Iraqi society, but to some extent revelling in them for short-term political gains.

As mentioned earlier, the disbanding of the Iraqi Army after the 2003 US invasion was one of the major reasons why the sectarian situation in certain parts of Iraq allowed groups such as ISIS to fester. The disbanding of an entire army, almost overnight, will have repercussions in any society, and this ill-conceived idea led to what we know today as the 'Sunni disenfranchisement' in the country after the toppling of the Hussein government. Bremer, the head of the CPA, a transitional governmental structure installed in Iraq after the US invasion to oversee the transition to a democratic process, was the architect of the disbandment. The strategic reasoning behind Bremer's decision, which was backed by then US President George W. Bush, remains contentious amidst academics and scholars to date. 'Well, the policy was to keep the (Iraqi) army intact. Didn't happen,' Bush apparently told his biographer according to James Pfiffner, professor of public policy at George Mason University, a US Army veteran and author of 'US Blunders in Iraq: De-Baathification and Disbanding the Army', one of the most incisive research papers on this decision. The paper showcases the abhorrent carelessness in decision-making and apparent disregard in recognizing the long-term repercussions on the local populations of Iraq. Bremer's decision to ignore the advice of the US Army, policy planners in the State Department and the Pentagon went unchallenged in the various inquiries that followed over the years as the war raged on, with his decision being at the centre of a lot of Iraq's challenges and hundreds, if not thousands, of civilian deaths. Pfiffner explains in numbers on why the decision to disband the army was central to providing the ideal environment for an entity like ISIS to thrive.

'Bremer, against the advice of the Army and the professional planners, issued CPA Order Number 2 on 23 May 2003, which dissolved the Iraqi security forces. The security forces included 3,85,000 in the armed forces, 2,85,000 in the Interior Ministry (police), and 50,000 in the presidential security units. Of course those in the police and military units that were Saddam's top enforcers (e.g. the Special Republican Guard) had to be barred from working in the government. But many officers in the Army were professional soldiers, and the rank and file enlisted soldiers constituted a source of stability and order. The disbanding threw hundreds of thousands out of work and immediately created a large pool of unemployed and armed men who felt humiliated, and hostile to the US occupiers,' Pfiffner writes.

The reasoning Bremer and his aide Walter Slocombe gave over their disbandment decision was flakey and bereft of long-term strategy. Both Bremer and Slocombe argued that the Iraqi Army had suffered a defeat so big that the institution had disbanded itself. This was further backed up by justifying that the destruction of the Iraqi Army's infrastructure and the garrisons being deserted by the Ba'athist fighters were grounds enough to officially disband the force, rendering thousands of trained soldiers jobless overnight.

President Bush's worry that expedited the process of this disbandment was the re-entry of Ba'athists loyal to Saddam back into either governance, military ranks, or worse, as leaders of potential military rule of the state. The 'quick fix' approach mixed with concerned interventions by some US generals made the situation worse, as multiple policy failures and an absence of clear foresight on not just the role of the army but also keeping sectarian divisions in check and a part of the political processes failed to gather enough attention beyond the military plans of the USA.

It can perhaps be argued that external military intervention in the Middle East cannot come up with any concrete strategies to appease the sectarian cracks that exist. And it is perhaps also arguable (albeit with this thinking probably being highly controversial) that the above postulation may still hold true even if the Middle East had not been split into the modern geographic boundaries we know of today by the Sykes–Picot Agreement of 1916, developed and signed in secret by France and Britain dividing their spheres of influence, aiding the defeat of the Ottoman Empire with the ending of the First

World War in 1918. Today, a lot of flak is given to London and Paris over the crassness of dividing the region not based on sociology or anthropology, but on whims and fancies of colonial requirements and strategic manoeuvring in order to keep exploitative influence, if not territory, post the independence of these newly formed states.

History As Crisis

British bureaucrat Mark Sykes and French diplomat François Georges-Picot were the men tasked to provide their last names to an agreement (officially known as the Asia Minor Agreement) made into and presented as official policy during the San Remo Conference in 1920. The accord divided the Middle East into what we mostly see today. The two warring schools of thought—one that blames Sykes–Picot for much of the discontent, violence and sectarian divisions and the other which sees such accusations as 'obsessions'—however do largely agree that peace in the region has to come from the very foundations of Arab thinking and social engineering, and not from interventions from foreign powers.

The Sykes–Picot agreement is also often blamed for the Israel–Palestine discord, one of the crux issues in the region that has not only fanned interstate rivalries and wars but also given birth to many of the major contemporary jihadist movements in the region. The friction between the Arab states and the Jewish homeland nestled in the Arab world has been pivotal in the rise of groups such as Hezbollah, Al Qaeda, Hamas and a slew of other smaller but divisive and dangerous extremist groups that are more often than not either covertly or blatantly supported by one or the other states in the Middle East.

While Sykes–Picot is blamed for many ills, including the Israeli–Palestinian conundrum, the argument that this ill-planned intervention by the British and French falls flat in front of the regional and tribal issues in the Middle East is not new. Most jihadist groups are privy to these dynamics, and exploit them to create discontent within communities. In July 2014, at the peak of the juggernaut of ISIS's territorial conquests in both Syria and Iraq, one of the group's many media propaganda arms, Al-Hayat Media Centre, released a video titled 'The End of Sykes–Picot'—one of the initial hints of what was to become an immense online effort by the group and its supporters—to spread propaganda and orchestrate recruitment drives attracting thousands of fighters from all parts of the world.

The video starts with ISIS fighter Abu Safiyya, allegedly from Chile, (a distance of 14,000 km separates Iraq and the South American nation) first and foremost showcasing the distance Safiyya himself must have travelled to join the so-called Islamic State. In the video, which runs for fifteen minutes, Safiyya is shown hoisting the black flag of the Islamic State on the border of Iraq and Syria, as per the Sykes–Picot treaty. He speaks in crisp English to the camera, and pronounces 'Picot' with a tinge of that famous Parisian tongue roll. He does not refer to the border as the border of the states of Iraq and Syria, but as the 'Sykes–Picot border'. Safiyya, with his Kalashnikov swung around his neck walks down towards a dusty board lying on the ground, which says 'Commandos Battalion Border', referring to the border guards. He then stands on the board, a sign of defiance and defeat of the state structure, proclaiming that the only borders here now are those of the Islamic State. He goes on to threaten the borders of not just Iraq, but Jordon, Lebanon and so on, as he walks towards a wall with a mural of the border markings separating Iraq and Syria. During this entire production, a specially created soundtrack runs in the background, a 'nasheed', or chant, in Arabic, specially produced by the ISIS propaganda machinery. As the music continues, Safiyya holds a deck of military patches, mostly from the Syrian Army and Iraqi Army, as trophies, showcasing the success of the conquests undertaken by ISIS. 'The soldiers, they took this off their uniforms and they threw the uniforms in the streets and they ran away . . . Cowards,' he says. 'There is no army in the world that can stand the soldiers of Islamic State, inshallah.' He continues, 'We are Muslims, there is only one country,' as the ISIS flag is unfurled on a pole on the 'Sykes–Picot border'. Safiyya then moves on to the signage around the border that have been stripped bare by ISIS, with trophy vehicles used by the Iraqi Army, some provided by the USA, displayed as signs of victory. Safiyya, strengthening the vision of this propaganda video, showcases white SUVs with 'Border Patrol' written on their sides and moves on to more, mostly US, machinery that ISIS had confiscated. The border patrol cars on display are either makes of Jeep or Ford, both US models, before moving on to showing destroyed or confiscated military Humvees given to the Iraqis by the Americans to take on ISIS. 'America has spent billions of dollars . . . they lost in Iraq, they lost in Afghanistan, they're going to lose in Syria also inshallah when they come, we'll be waiting for them,' he proclaims.[1]

Safiyya then moves on from war spoils to a prison, where ISIS is keeping prisoners they gathered after the takeover of

Mosul. In the small room behind a steel door, around fifteen men sit across the room, in a square, the shape of the prison cell. 'Some of them are Shia . . . some of them are Yazidi. For those who don't know what Yazidi is, they're those who worship the devil,' he explains, and asks the Yazidis specifically to raise their hands to identify them. Later in the video, Safiyya is seen on a pickup truck looking at a solitary building, which he identifies as a police station. A few seconds later, the building blows up. It's unclear from the video whether it is the same building where the Yazidi and Shia prisoners were held. The video ends with Safiyya and another man mocking the West, sitting inside a US-made Ford truck, with two children, boys roughly between the ages of three and five, playing in the back of the truck. 'I will say that now Syria and Iraq became one country [reference to the caliphate] and the other countries are on the way,' the driver of the truck is shown saying. The video ends with the same man asking a question, 'A question to Obama: did you prepare enough diapers for your soldiers or not?' The video ends with the men, and the children, talking and yelling, showing that the children were known to the men and were probably brought in specifically for this propaganda production.

Sykes–Picot did no favours to the people of the region, populations that were intricately loyal to their tribes and socio-ethnic backgrounds. The umbrella arguments in contemporary political discussions that Sykes–Picot has some sort of exclusive stake in current crisis hotspots in the Middle East, including the rise of global jihadist movements due to the prolonged presence of Western powers in the region, predominantly USA and Britain, is a lazy take at best. Taking a microscope to the Middle East and its socio-cultural and socio-ethnic fabrics will perhaps only highlight that the barriers between Shias and Sunnis, and even within those groups, would in all likelihood have kept the region on edge.

Eminent British journalist and Arabist Patrick Cockburn in a 2013 essay[2] in the wake of the Syrian civil war asked whether the current bout of political strife in the Middle East would be the end of the Sykes–Picot arrangement as we know it today. This would mean states with their current geographic borders collapsing into smaller states, or just being engulfed by civil strife with national structures being either compromised or left in control over only certain territories for a prolonged period of time, escalating the possibilities of a state, such as Syria today, losing its Sykes–Picot era geographic identity.

The fact that Cockburn's ideations in 2013 are poles apart from the situation and realities today underscores the fragility of the Middle East, and illustrates the extreme difficulty in both predicting the future political course of the region and in the US, British and French cases, engineering change towards democratic and federalist political structures.

'What will the new order in the Middle East look like? This should be Turkey's great moment in the region: it has a powerful military, a prospering economy and a well-established government. It is allied to Saudi Arabia and Qatar in supporting the Syrian opposition and is on good terms with the US,' Cockburn wrote. Today, like every day over the past many decades, no one has clarity on what the 'new order' in the Middle East will look like.

The counter to the Sykes–Picot argument on stability and security of the region highlights the role of the minimally discussed San Remo Conference, which led to the Treaty of Sèvres in August 1920.

The San Remo Conference often loses its importance in the shadow of arguments surrounding the Sykes–Picot Agreement. However, it was as important an event, and perhaps contributed much more to the modern post-Ottoman shaping of the region than Sykes–Picot. The conference was held in San Remo, a commune kissing the Mediterranean Sea on Italy's border with France, and attended by the then leaders of Great Britain, France, and Italy along with representatives from Greece, Belgium, and Japan. An agenda was set to abolish the remains of the defeated Ottoman Empire as a consequence of World War I. The end result, the Treaty of Sèvres, officially dismantled the Ottoman territories and created 'mandates' in favour of both Britain and France. The treaty divided the Ottoman Province of Syria into two; the northern half that includes modern Syria and Lebanon was mandated to France and the southern half, Palestine, to Britain. The post-WWI independence of these regions was highly constricted, playing fast and loose with the term 'independence' itself; the divisions were based on influence, of what London and Paris wanted the political future of these kaleidoscopes of sectarian and tribally-divided quasi-states to be, or whatever the two colonialist powers could be bothered with at that time.

Both Britain and France looked for a conceptual reformation according to Western understandings and discourses of political thought of the largely tribal dynamics of the region. The San Remo mandates, arguably naively, looked for 'political maturity', and installed 'mandatory power' until said aims of post-colonial control were achieved. The divisions in the Middle East's geography usually do not attest to the ground realities of how the society is divided, between Shias and Sunnis, and the Kurds, Yazidis, Christians, and other minority groups. While it is clear that Saudi Arabia led by the royal family also known as the House of Saud is the seat of Sunni Islam, with both Mecca and Medina under its helm, the post-1979 revolution Iran under the all-encompassing spiritual rule of the Supreme Leader Ayatollah and his Islamic Revolutionary Guard Corps (IRGC) is home to the seat of Shiite Islam. Both these poles of power in the region are single-handedly responsible for both the social and political architecture of the post-colonial, modern Middle East, and much of the social engineering that still takes place in the region happens predominantly due to the constant ideological struggles between the Shias and the Sunnis.

The current structures of states in the Middle East have always remained under duress, and for some, Western support has been critical to their survivability. While US, British, and French interventions in the region have been historically aligned to the policies and narratives of that era, it is the Americans and the British that have had more influence over the politics and stability of the region than the others, extending from the Cold War between the USA and erstwhile Soviet Union until the latter's collapse around the same time as the First Gulf War. The policies and battles fought between the leaders of the Middle East and Western powers were always narrow in ideation and the achievements that their policies wished to win, and this remains so to date. 11 September, of course, was a turning point, when historically poor policies from Sykes–Picot to USA's installation of Mohammad Reza Pahlavi, a pro-Western and the last monarch of the House of Pahlavi, as the Shah of Iran from 1941 until his ouster at the hands of Iran's conservatives in February 1979, to the Libyan misadventures by the USA and European allies in 2011.

The rise of the likes of Al Qaeda in the late 1980s and ISIS during the Syrian civil war, and smaller jihadist factions fed on these interventionist narratives to bolster their support base, relying on fake descriptions, news, propaganda, and playing on social insecurities on safety and economic destitution, to recruit fighters that have little to nothing to lose, and often in a bizarre sense, find safety and refuge by joining jihadist ranks themselves. The disparity between what was going to happen in Syria and Iraq following a balmy day in December 2010, and 2,700 kilometers away in a small and sleepy town of central Tunisia on the coast of the warm Mediterranean Sea, were not predicted by anyone, and one Mohamed Bouazizi, a lanky, twenty-six-year-old humble fruit seller was to once again challenge the very essence of the government, policy, history, politics, and society of the most volatile region in the world.

The Arab Spring

The era from 2008 to 2011 was one that moulded many of the political and societal upheavals in the Middle East, out of which many of the crises of both overthrowing of current rulers and emergence of new non-state militant actors came into being. In Tunisia, Bouazizi one day was selling fruit on his cart when he was confronted by the local police, who told him that he was selling fruit illegally and did not have the correct permits to be doing so. After Bouazizi protested and refused to indulge them, and was publicly humiliated by the officials, he made his way to the local administration's office and set himself on fire, succumbing to burn injuries later on. Bouazizi's actions started a public outcry in Tunisia against corruption and overreach of systems that harassed and intimidated the common man on a daily basis. This largely localized protest by a street seller set off a chain reaction in the Middle East, with protests by citizens against long-standing dictatorial and corrupt regimes springing up in countries such as Egypt, Turkey, Syria and in smaller hotspots in a host of Gulf nations.

These protests gained momentum globally, with support pouring in from Western nations that saw this as a potential moment in history where long-standing status-quos of the region, usually supported by Western nations themselves, were to collapse and a new dawn would emerge led by a people's uprising, resulting in democratic processes being incorporated into the political DNA of the region. The then US President Barack Obama put his weight behind the protests in Tahrir Square in Cairo, which became a focal point of the movement, and Tahrir Square, a global icon of a revolution against corruption and the dictatorial rule of now former Egyptian leader Hosni Mubarak.

'There are very few moments in our lives where we have the privilege to witness history taking place,' Obama said in February 2011 after Mubarak stepped down as a result of the Tahrir Square protests. 'This is one of those moments. This is one of those times. The people of Egypt have spoken, their voices have been heard, and Egypt will never be the same.'[1]

What happened next in Egypt, bouncing to democracy and choosing a hard-line Muslim Brotherhood government, much to US displeasure and coming back to a military autocracy only months later, perhaps showed Obama's fallacies in being yet another US President who did not understand the region.

The Arab Spring also divided analysis into two sections, between those who saw the revolution as a pivotal point in not just the Middle East's contemporary history but one that would cause a wake in global politics, and the others who thought the support these revolutions got to uproot existing governance structures was without any long-term understanding of the complexities that fester under the region's bonnet.

The challenges of the Arab Spring were much larger, both to understand and react to, than any other such event in history due to one single defining factor. The Internet. Similar to the First Gulf War being the first conflict beamed live into people's living rooms via cable television, the advent of the Internet and the mobility provided by smartphones brought Tahrir Square not just to people with the privilege of owning a television with a cable connection but also to people in the remotest parts of the planet who were able to stream, read, and listen to not just global news but happenings on the ground that were available live without a media organization as their provider. The Arab Spring was the revolution of social media. Twitter, Facebook, and other such mediums took centre stage for people to watch, read, comment, opine, and perhaps more importantly, use this technology and ease of connection to organize themselves with relative ease.

Zeynep Tufekci—an associate professor at the University of North Carolina, USA, who in her excellent book *Twitter and Tear Gas: The Power and Fragility of Networked Protest* researched and argued on the Tahrir Square protests and the ensuing political crisis that consumed Egypt—tracks the development of networked digital communications from the higher classes to the lower, allowing the latter to use this tool, once too expensive for them to use, to challenge political and economic repression that they may have suffered for decades on end.

'The French salons and coffeehouses of the nineteenth century were mostly limited to middle- or upper-class men, as were digital technologies in their early days,' she writes, 'but as digital technology has rapidly become less expensive, it has just as rapidly spread to poorer groups. It is the new town square, the water cooler, the village well and the urban coffeehouse, but also much more. This isn't because people leave behind race, gender, and social class online, and this isn't because the online sphere is one with no impact from the physical world. Quite the opposite, such dimensions of the human experience are reproduced and play a significant role in the networked public sphere as well. The difference is the reconfigured logic of how and where we can interact, with whom, and at what scale and visibility.'[2]

The use of these platforms for 'revolutions' was unexpected for the said platforms themselves and even the governments realized their need and importance in an ad hoc manner, as the Arab Spring spread. President Obama saw this as an opportunity, and suggested to Twitter during these protests that the company postpone any scheduled maintenance downtimes. Social media, specifically Twitter, was suddenly at the forefront of an event it was perhaps not designed for, or did not expect to find itself in the midst of events where it was being used to overthrow governments. At this point, the White House decided to use this opportunity to further the cause of democracy in the region. This idealism, which ran down from the Oval Office to prominent figureheads from the President's adviser Ben Rhodes to the then US Ambassador to the UN, Samantha Power, was to become one of the most misjudged and misinterpreted policy decisions in the modern history of US politics.

The Narratives

On 20 January 2017, a business magnate and property dealer, who was to parachute himself into the midst of US politics by decimating the Republican Party's ethos and one of the world's oldest democracies' moral compasses, became the world's most powerful man. President Donald J. Trump introduced a new era of uncertainty while critical US operations beyond its borders were taking place, including the war in Afghanistan, and the newly-initiated military operations against ISIS in Syria and Iraq.

During his swearing-in, the so-called Islamic State was in geographic recession. From holding a sizeable territory across the sovereign borders of both Iraq and Syria, today the group's influence is concentrated largely around Deir Ezzor, on the banks of the Euphrates where the desert and river meet, giving a limited landscape for life to flourish. The US aim against ISIS can be described with a term used by Glenn A. Fine, Principal Deputy Inspector General performing the duties of the Inspector General, US Department of Defense, who called for an 'enduring defeat' of ISIS and its franchises.

As early as mid-2017, the narratives around the defeat of the ISIS caliphate were starting to get promoted in the press. In an interview in October 2018, President Trump told journalists that ISIS had been defeated. 'We've defeated ISIS. ISIS is defeated in all of the areas that we fought ISIS, and that would have never happened under President Obama. In fact, it is going the other way. And I think we fought extremely effectively on everything I've wanted to do,'[1] he gloated of the achievement of defeating Daesh under his command.

Both the rise of ISIS and the fight against it came at a time when the world was on the edge of major political and ideological shifts, led by the US elections of 2016, which saw the overthrow of traditional Washington politics with the defeat of Democratic candidate Hillary Clinton, who lost the polls despite a strong ecosystem of understanding the politics of her country with former two-time president Bill Clinton at her side. On counterterrorism and the place of the US military in the world, both Trump and Obama at certain points during their campaigns had similar ideas for their targeted electorates with perhaps only the interpretations and means to the end being different.

In May 2014, speaking to a group of young US military cadets at West Point, New York, Obama highlighted terrorism as the 'most direct threat to America at home and abroad'. 'America must always lead on the world stage. If we don't, no one else will. The military that you have joined is and always will be the backbone of that leadership,' he said. 'But US military action cannot be the only—or even primary—component of our leadership in every instance. Just because we have the best hammer does not mean that every problem is a nail.'[2] This speech, the views in which Obama had also championed during his pre-2008 campaign, came almost exactly three years after a special US military raid deep inside Pakistan, in the town of Abbottabad, killed the chief of Al Qaeda, Osama bin Laden, merely a month before ISIS announced its caliphate.

The interpretation of this statement by analysts and the press was of Obama's views being against the USA being a 'policeman' of the world. In another instance, Obama chimed in that the USA perhaps faces unreasonable expectations from every corner of the globe, where it is criticized for both taking military action against global injustice and not taking military action at all. These discussions in the USA have been part of its discourse for decades, specifically after the Second World War, when Washington designed global security umbrellas that it could lead against its foes, and with aims to prevent a third World War by taking on communism head-on at that point of time itself.

After the fall of the erstwhile Soviet Union and the subsequent end of the Cold War, Islamist-terrorism emitting from the Middle East started to take precedence as the main 'nail' of US foreign policy. The late 1980s and early 1990s also saw the rise of groups such as Al Qaeda, formed by bin Laden, heir of a rich Saudi business family. During this period, Al Qaeda formulated its structures, spreading its ideologies across the Middle East and building a network that allowed it to target US interests in any part of the world.

The rise of the Islamic State was different. The fact that thousands of Muslims from around the world answered Baghdadi's call to come and help in the creation of a new radical jihadist state offered a level of success that even Al Qaeda would be jealous of. The switch in the narrative from the fear of post-9/11 Al Qaeda to these new kids on the block who were not hiding out in the destitute mountainous regions of Tora Bora in Afghanistan, but were openly, and proudly, propagating their ideology, control of territory and most importantly, violence, changed the dynamics.

The geographic hold under ISIS in both Iraq and Syria was always going to be a fragile affair. While it remains one of the greatest non-state militant actors' coups in the history of modern terrorism, showcasing their capabililty to develop a quasi state, the transition of the group from an insurgency into a proto-state and now heading back to an insurgency raises more questions than answers on what the world's response against such threats has been over the past decade or more.

The presence of both sectarian divisions and geopolitical chinwagging made sure that ISIS, despite its ultra-violent form of jihad, not only survived but was also used in the regional smorgasbord of power struggles. During its formative years, the flow of foreign fighters into Syria, a country bordered by the likes of Iraq, Lebanon and Turkey, and a geography not the easiest to penetrate by land as far as movement of jihadist fighters is concerned, begged a question: How did hundreds of fighters from Europe, northern Africa, other parts of the Middle East, and as far as Canada and Australia, manage to enter the Syrian theatre with relative ease between the periods 2014–16? Who, at the end of the day, decided to turn a blind eye?

The answer to the initial buildup of fighters largely lies on the 822-km-long Syria-Turkey border, and the foreign policy aims of the Turkish state under the leadership of its authoritarian President Recep Tayyip Erdogan of what some call a 'neo-Ottoman' renaissance, looking to reinvigorate the clout of the erstwhile Ottoman empire and Turkey's place as the leader of the Islamic world, instead of its not-so-close neighbour Saudi Arabia. Ankara's thinking during this period was based on its own domestic politics, and issues relating to the Kurdish populations of the Middle East. The Kurds, sprawled across the region and considered the world's largest ethnic group without their own state, have been living amidst the wide variety of sectarian and geopolitical strife in the region for decades. For Turkey, groups such as the Kurdistan Workers' Party (PKK) are seen as major threats to its sovereignty, and disallowing the Kurds to set up their own state remains one of the top foreign policy and regional goals for them. However, this is not easy, as Kurds themselves constitute more than 18 per cent of Turkey's total population of 82 million people, a significant bite of the country's demographics despite their minority status. Nonetheless, the PKK is recognized as a terror group by the USA and many other countries (India has yet to blacklist the PKK as a terror group). Cohesively, the PKK is not a declared terror group via a United Nations resolution.

Considering Turkey's regional manoeuvring of challenging Saudi Arabia as the chieftain of Sunni Islam not just in the region but globally, Ankara on some level saw the crisis in Syria and the rise of both Al Qaeda-aligned groups and ISIS in Syria as events where it could perhaps gain a strong grasp of the narrative away from Riyadh. The vast Turkish-Syrian border was the number one people smuggling route for both foreign fighters trying to get in and those trying to flee the conflict. Today, it is home to more than three million refugees.

The porous nature of the Turkish border and the ease with which smugglers operated perhaps had a tinge of complacency from the Turks' part to try and tame the Kurdish narrative as well, which by this time in the war against ISIS was getting an outpouring of support from the West which heralded the Kurds at the forefront of almost all ground battles. While the Western coalition provided air support and troops under the guise of advisers, Turkey was, according to some accounts, allowing ISIS fighters to go through its borders into Syria. Human trafficking became a cottage industry of deplorable proportions during these times, with pro-ISIS persons trying to get in and Syrian civilians that had access to some money trying their best to get out. A mix of opportunism and corruption also came into play, as soldiers posted on the border became part of the 'cut' economy, where they would get a portion of the money from the traffickers themselves for looking the other way while this migration took place. One of the ways in which travellers looking to join ISIS in Syria made their way across was handing over their passports to the Turkish authorities for destruction on the border. The non-existence of any documentation was seen as a way of 'citizenship' to the Islamic State; they would then be allowed to step into Syria from Turkey but would now be recognized officially as ISIS and not the citizens of their birth nations. This would literally imply, in a hypothetical yet fully plausible way, that Turkish soldiers who conducted operations against certain jihadist groups in 2017 and 2018 may well have risked their own lives and fought the very same people whom they allowed to cross the border.

Meanwhile, the northern flanks of Syria remain much more complicated today despite the fall of Aleppo as ISIS continues to fan its global propaganda machinery.

ISIS and South Asia: A Smorgasbord of Threats and Fear

India and the Middle East have ties between their people going back thousands of years. The civilizational bonds between these two regions are mammoth, and their languages, cultures, history and people-to-people contact are part of everyone's daily lives, knowingly or unknowingly. For much of the past few decades, while having strong ties with most regional state powers, New Delhi's interests towards the larger Gulf area have been two-fold. First, and foremost, is demographics. More than five million Indians work in the larger Middle East region.[1] While a sizeable number of these today work in the high-skilled labour market, majority still work in the low-skilled labour market, with construction and other such labour-intensive jobs being largely manned by Indians travelling to the Gulf and so on. This means that the Indian government on a daily basis is responsible for the protection, and upholding of the rights of a population that is larger in size than Finland. Beyond the sheer numbers at play, these seven million Indian citizens constitute a big chunk of India's overseas remittances pumped into the economy every year, money that workers abroad send back to their homes here. In 2017, India was the highest recipient of remittance at $69 billion as per World Bank figures,[2] which is more than the country's annual defence budget.

Both the seven million citizens and the billions of dollars in hard currency infused into the economy every year are of very high interest to the country's national security. In the 1990s, India's economy was a fraction of its current form, with remittances in 1991, the year Indian economy was liberalized, standing at a mere $3 billion.[3] During much of the 1990s, Indian clout in the Gulf was minimal, and India was largely seen as a labour provider. However, the story has been turned on its head over the past ten years. India's strategic importance in the world as a fast-growing economic power and one whose words carry weight in global discourse has orchestrated a paradigm shift on how major Arab capitals such as Abu Dhabi and Riyadh look at the country. In the 1990s, it would have been an unheard of event if the United Arab Emirates (UAE) or Saudi Arabia would have deported a terrorism suspect wanted by India. Fast-forward a few years, and the UAE and Saudi alike have deported suspects that India has highlighted in an expedited manner, sometimes doing so within days.

In 2018, the UAE deported around a dozen people to India who were suspected of pro-ISIS activities. 'There are no grey areas, we need to tackle this (ISIS) threat and nobody is immune. If you think you are immune (and) you are going to be negligent, you are going to be hit,' Dr Anwar Mohammed Gargash, UAE's Minister of State for Foreign Affairs, said during his visit to New Delhi in July 2018.[4] Similarly, in 2017, Riyadh had deported a thirty-seven-year-old man from Rajasthan at the behest of India's investigative agencies due to his alleged pro-ISIS links.[5]

Not just the Gulf, India's goodwill in the larger Middle East region is robust and benefits its future security requirements not just on counterterrorism, but regional cooperation and bolstering its presence in the Indian Ocean Region (IOR). To calibrate its outreach with the UAE and Saudi Arabia, New Delhi is also involved in connectivity projects such as the development of the Chabahar port in Iran, which will not only give landlocked Afghanistan another access other than Pakistani ports for its economy, but will also connect Central Asian markets with South Asia. The third pole of regional power, Israel, has found an ideological and political 'better half' for itself in India over the past five years. Prime Minister Narendra Modi became the first Indian prime minister to visit Israel in July 2017, twenty-five years after diplomatic ties between the two countries were established. This 'plural' approach to the region, and the fact that India does not wade into regional matters and pontificate to states on how to conduct their affairs and allows all three poles of power, Israel, Saudi Arabia, and Iran, who are fundamentally against each other, to accept each other's robust relations with India in a non-partisan manner—from a Middle East perspective, is nothing short of a miracle.

Iraq's then Prime Minister Haider al-Abadi landed in the besieged city of Mosul on the eve of 10 July 2017 to announce the defeat of the so-called Islamic State. 'I announce from here the end and the failure and the collapse of the terrorist state of falsehood and terrorism which the terrorist Daesh announced from Mosul,'[6] he said in a speech picked up by the international media. India had, under quiet quarters, been supporting Baghdad in its anti-ISIS rally. Iraq's Ambassador to India, Fakhri Hassan

Al Issa, in 2017 highlighted the fact that the Indian government had offered military help, including training and supply of equipment.[7] The Iraqi embassy building, in one of New Delhi's diplomatic quarters, sported a banner on the front façade announcing and celebrating the defeat of ISIS in the city of Mosul.

India offering help to the Iraqis comes as a change of historical posturing as well. During the start of the Iraq war against the regime of Saddam in the aftermath of the 9/11 attacks on the USA, the then Indian Prime Minister Atal Bihari Vajpayee was on the cusp of sending in troops to the Middle East at the USA's behest. He faced pressure, oddly from his own colleagues in the Bharatiya Janata Party (BJP) as well as from the likes of Lal Krishna Advani, the then Deputy Prime Minister. Vajpayee, known for his consensus-based politics, held consultations with the opposition parties and eventually informed the USA, much to the George W. Bush administration's dismay, that New Delhi in fact will not be participating in this coalition.

Had India under Vajpayee done so, the country's foreign policy approach towards the region would have been drastically different today on all fronts ranging from economic to counterterrorism. Understanding this paradigm of non-intervention is, to some extent, important in understanding why a terror group such as ISIS failed to develop a foothold in the country. In fact, not just ISIS, but the likes of Al Qaeda and so on have also failed to develop any sort of lasting institutional presence. Why? To answer this question, we have to understand multiple policy and societal decisions India took during its formation, specifically on matters of foreign policy relating to the Muslim world. But first and foremost, to put it all in some context, we need to revisit the Non-Aligned Movement (NAM) and the kind of reputation it developed as part of its outreach during the leadership of India's first Prime Minister, Jawaharlal Nehru.

The Non-Aligned Movement, as most of us know, was spearheaded by the likes of India, Egypt and others as a group of countries that refused to officially park themselves in one of the two power blocs leading the world into a heightened sense of armed crisis during the Cold War, as the USA and erstwhile Soviet Union took on each other over who would become the sole global hegemon. New Delhi maintained, beyond Nehru as well, that it did not take sides. However, as the years went by, and geopolitical intricacies, specifically as US support for Pakistan developed, it started to align more and more with Moscow to safeguard its own strategic interests. While the NAM still persists today, it is a mere shadow of its former self, with realities of global politics trumping its initial idealistic agendas. However, much of today's success can arguably be traced back to Nehru's policies and personal charisma alike. During the formative years of NAM and Nehru's leadership, he visited Syria twice, first in 1957 and a second time in 1960. On the latter trip, Nehru was welcomed at the airport by then Syrian leader Shukri al-Quwatli accompanied by 'tens of thousands of people', chanting 'welcome to the hero of world peace' and 'long live the leader of Asia'. This gravitas and cementing of India's name done during the early periods of India's independence get credit for the successful diplomatic manoeuvring in the Middle East possible today.

Nonetheless, despite the NAM forum and its idea being past its expiration date, for New Delhi, it has proven useful in building capital in the Middle East and accessing the complicated and tribal structures of the region. India's Foreign Secretary,

Vijay Gokhale, at various public platforms, has reiterated a new mantra for the Indian approach to the world, that of 'strategic autonomy'.[8] This terminology, which some call a NAM for the modern era where India has ambitions of being a superpower, has managed to build vastly upon NAM itself despite its larger failures, but visible successes in the Middle East. Gokhale has offered India's 'new' stance with some theatre attached to it. He has said that today despite still following the basic tenants of the Non-Aligned Movement, India is now aligned. Not to a power bloc, or an ideological bloc as it was during the Cold War, but to India's interests, requirements, and needs. Aligned to actors who can fulfil India's economic and security requirements.

How this plays out in the Middle East, and why the region which saw the rise of ISIS and other prevailing conflicts is turning out to be a success story for Indian diplomacy is an episode worth watching. In fact, the war against ISIS itself provides an excellent canvas to highlight how India's outreach to the region during these times of crisis has not been good for its own security but by extension, the security of the entire South Asian region itself.

India's approach to the Syrian civil war has been through the nooks and cracks of diplomatic grey areas, where New Delhi has not taken an overt stance against the regime of President Assad. Since the Arab Spring protests started in Syria in 2010, and were later taken over by a wide variety of interest groups including Islamist terrorists such as Al Qaeda in Iraq which, as mentioned earlier, morphed into ISIS and anti-Assad factions ranging from local militia groups to defectors from the Syrian Arab Army. Despite the country going through unimaginable crisis and observing a near collapse of the Assad government, which was kept propped up thanks to the Russian and Iranian backing he received, India amidst one of the greatest crisis of the twenty-first century kept its embassy in Damascus open (barring a few months when the Ambassador was recalled due to the security situation being very bleak, and the mission being maintained by a chargé d'affaires).

Ambassador V.P. Haran, who served as the top diplomat of India in Damascus from 2009–13, watched the Arab Spring unfold from his embassy on the capital's posh Ibn Al Haytham Avenue. Haran was direct in his finger-pointing on the Syrian crisis and the precarious rise of groups such as Al Qaeda. By the time Haran left, ISIS had not been officially declared as a proto-state by Baghdadi. Haran said that the crisis in Syria was instigated by foreign powers, especially Gulf states, Al Qaeda and, perhaps a little bizarrely, Al Jazeera, Qatar's national television outlet.[9] He had also highlighted the fact that diplomats in the country were aware of tunnels being used by Al Qaeda operatives as smuggling highways and for terrorists to make their way into the city without being detected.

India's approach towards the Syrian crisis has involved subtly supporting the Assad regime, despite often being contradictory to its own policies. For example, New Delhi has made repeated calls for all issues around the crisis to be solved via talks and negotiations, highlighting the fact that military solutions are not viable.[10] However, at the same time, during former Indian President Pranab Mukherjee's trip to Jordan, Israel, and Palestine, the then Secretary (East), Ministry of External Affairs (MEA), Anil Wadhwa, while taking questions said, 'There's no military solution to the Syrian crisis. The long-term solution should be political.' Then, when asked specifically about India's position on Russian military intervention and air strikes, Wadhwa said, 'The Indian position is that the Russian military involvement in Syria is to halt the advances of the Islamic State.'[11] (It was also during this trip that, while addressing the Israeli Knesset (parliament), Mukherjee had said, 'Indian population enjoy the taste of Hummus', but had instead pronounced Hummus as Hamas, the Palestinian terror group, sending the parliamentarians into a tizzy).

Despite global pressures, India continued to deal with the Assad regime throughout the rise and fall of the Islamic State story. Diplomatic delegations between both the countries continued, as New Delhi banked on its decades-long good relations with the Assad family. In 2016, India abstained from a United Nations vote on a ceasefire in Syria tabled by Canada during the siege of Aleppo. Indian diplomatic sources were quoted by the Press Trust of India (PTI) as saying that the resolution mixed humanitarian and political interests, which did not sit well with India's 'traditional approach'. 'The resolution had elements addressing the humanitarian situation mixed with political viewpoints of the sponsors which made for an uncomfortable cocktail. Consequently we abstained in line with our approach that is for a delineation of humanitarian issues from the politics of a situation,' the sources were quoted as saying.[12]

Beyond the historical ties, it is also entirely probable that India was worried that a sudden decapitation of the Assad leadership in Syria would possibly lead to wider meltdown in the Middle East. This was observed by the world in Libya, when in 2011 NATO-initiated Operation Unified Protector, which saw longtime Libyan dictator Muammar Gaddafi's regime ousted as Western powers installed a no-fly zone over the North African state, enforcing United Nations Security Council resolutions 1970 and 1973 (where India sat on the UNSC during this period) concerning the ensuing civil war in the state. European air power installed itself over the skies of Libya as rebels close to Western powers and those fighting against the Gaddafi autocracy fought to 'liberate' the country from the Arab leaders. New Delhi was averse to this action despite a brief period of flirtation with the UN's Responsibility to Protect (R2P) norm when India abstained in the votes for resolution 1973.[13] Eventually, it went back to its traditional diplomacy postures and joined the likes of Russia and China in criticizing the justifications behind conducting air strikes against the Gaddafi regime. India's then Foreign Minister S.M. Krishna had the same stance to what India later did in Syria and said that the military interventionism should stop and called upon Gaddafi and the rebels to talk to each other to iron out the differences. New Delhi once again highlighted its stance on combining political and humanitarian narratives to justify military strikes against a state, fearing political vacuums leading to strains on its own interests but also creating significant challenges in the larger Arab world.

What happened next in Libya impressively vindicated India's stance. NATO, the USA and other supporters of the Libyan war that backed their advances on the pretext of a fast deteriorating political condition in the country around the Arab Spring and the need to prevent all-out anarchy in the state which is close to mainland European shores struggled to keep Libya away from becoming the new hotspot for Islamist jihadists. While this political collapse took place, ISIS, at its peak, started to move in and form one of its first major 'offshore' presences as a group. Thus, success of this movement was the fall of Sirte, a city located between the capital Tripoli and rebel centre Benghazi, which fell under the control of the Islamic State.

For ISIS, Libya was a fertile ground and conducive to cementing its position there. As mentioned above, the Gaddafi vs rebels fight became even more rabid with intra-militia competition to stake claim over territory, resources and people. Researchers Jason Pack, Rhiannon Smith and Karim Mezran found that the tyranny unleashed by rebels in the country created a fertile ground for ISIS to thrive in, and this tyranny was ingrained in the institutional malaise of the country.[14] The state's structures and decades of political apathy were the grounds on which ISIS built up its *wilayat* (governorate) in Sirte, and as discussed earlier, was also how ISIS expanded in both Syria and Iraq.

Libya's demise and the rise of ISIS also ultimately came to haunt New Delhi once again. In 2015, four Indians, including medical professionals, were held captive by ISIS around Sirte. While two of them were released within days, the others took nearly two years to gain freedom. Under what terms and conditions they were released, and whether ransoms were paid remains unknown.

Dr Ramamurthy Kosanam, originally from Hyderabad, Andhra Pradesh, had been living in Libya as a medical professional for eighteen years before the civil war broke out. As the war spread and ISIS took over those parts of the country, Kosanam, while attempting to leave the region, was stopped at a checkpoint set up by ISIS and held captive. His profession was to become his bane, as his prolonged captivity inside an ISIS camp would have a lot to do with the fact that he was capable of treating wounded ISIS soldiers. Kosanam also highlighted some details of his interactions with ISIS fighters, saying that he was forced to watch pro-ISIS propaganda videos that highlighted their gory and violent methods of dealing with adversaries in areas such as Iraq, Nigeria and Libya. He was also taught about Islam, the Quran and how to pray according to ISIS tenants. Kosanam, in his public statements, also provided brief insights gained from further interactions with ISIS fighters, saying that they were mostly young, seemed well-educated and were up-to-date with global news and what was happening around them, and perhaps more interestingly, they were aware of India's 'education and economic' prowess and that they, ISIS, were 'interested' in India. 'They [Islamic State] are interested in India, they want to spread their ideology in other parts of the world . . . including India,' Kosanam said. He added that he saw suicide bombers being used by ISIS in Libya as young as ten years old.

Kosanam's release was, perhaps, by pure luck. On one of the days of his captivity, after being shot both in the arms and legs over the past months, the Libyan military backed by the Western-backed interim government in Tripoli was heard close to the building he was being held in. Risking being killed by ISIS, he shouted for help, and him along with four others were saved from the building they were being held in.

The narrative of the demise of ISIS, and in effect, that of the so-called Islamic State had started to appear in primarily Western discourse months before Abadi's trip to Mosul. In 2014, ISIS had taken over Iraq's second largest city with relative ease, and their leader, Baghdadi, took to the Great Mosque of al-Nuri in the city centre to announce the institutionalization of their proto-state. Between 2014 and 2016, ISIS conquered territory at a perilous pace in both Iraq and Syria, setting up governorates to install its rules and laws according to the organization's interpretations of Islam.

Diminished Territory, Weakened Brand?

The rapid decline of the ISIS caliphate has raised many questions over the structure that the group would take after their loss of territory. Researchers have studied available data and examined scenarios looking at the fate of other global insurgency movements in the past, along with local sectarian dynamics in Syria and Iraq. These methodologies, in some ways, have redesigned the scholarly debate around the topic of terrorism itself. However, they have their own limitations when used to study IS. The grey areas under which the proto-state operated offered no compelling and targeted arguments on the future form of the organization, both political and strategic.

The fall of Mosul was a pivotal point in the war against ISIS, with the recapture of the city that ended with ISIS destroying the al-Nuri mosque itself. Moving forward from July 2017, ISIS has lost its territorial controls at a rapid pace, as the Iraqi military, backed by a collective of anti-ISIS militias and US-led Western coalition under the programme 'Inherent Resolve', liberated one city after the other (See Figures 1 and 2). In Syria,

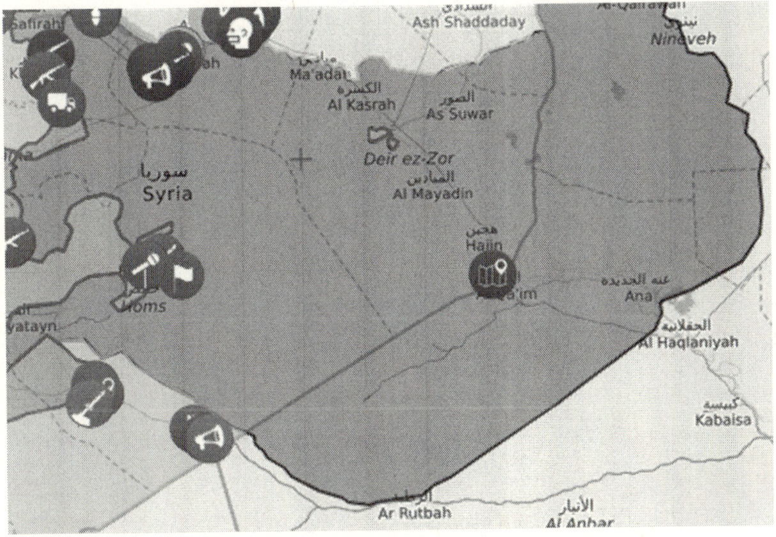

(Figure 1: ISIS territorial control [grey] in May 2017)[1]

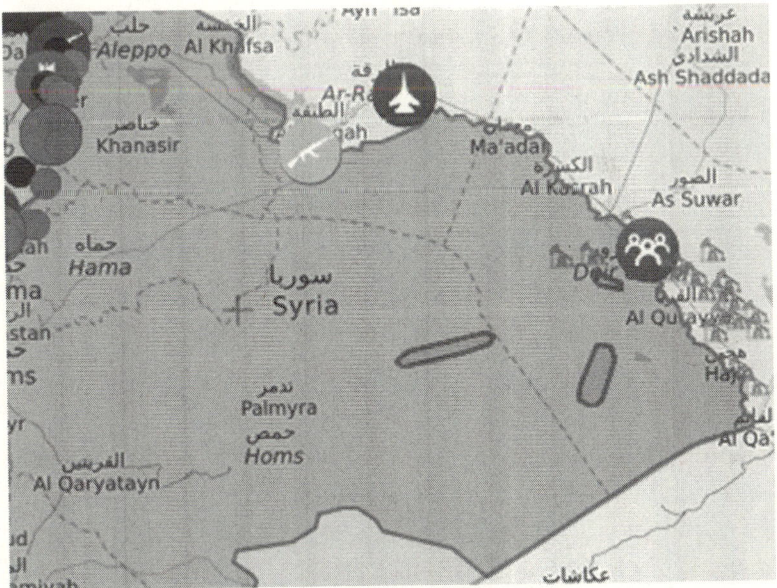

(Figure 2: ISIS territorial control [grey] in April 2019)[2]

while the optics were politically different—with Russia and Iran backing Syrian President Assad's regime—territorial loss for ISIS, including the recent loss of its de facto capital Raqqa, diminished its influence. Perhaps, more importantly, its global narrative has also weakened.[3]

All the debates on the 'end' of ISIS are based on a false equation that defines a long-term military victory over the group as a strategic win. It is imperative to remember that ISIS started as an insurgency, born out of Al Qaeda's attempts to set up a strong presence in Iraq under Al Qaeda in Iraq's (AQI) first leader and ideologue, Zarqawi.[4] Relinquishing territory back to the Iraqi and Syrian governments has been a significant moral setback for ISIS. This can be measured by its constant and often increasing media output, trying to maintain the morale of not only its fighters on the ground, but also the important online support base the organization has skilfully cultivated over the past four years.

These said losses over the past year, which include critical cities and towns such as Mosul, Kirkuk, Tikrit Fallujah, Ramadi, Tal Afar, Deir Ezzor, Albu Kamal and now Raqqa, are in themselves a significant study of local politics and socio-cultural and ethnic realities. They hold clues to what the future of ISIS might be. The loss of Raqqa means ISIS will largely be concentrated only in Syria, and predominantly the country's desert regions in Deir Ezzor. Facing this situation, ISIS is expected to transform itself from its current proto-state structure back to its original organizational form, which was of an insurgency movement. Even as the Iraqi military has made progress against ISIS, there are signs that the political vacuum in the country that initially led ISIS to succeed in capturing territory is re-emerging.[5] Members of Sunni tribal militias, in the aftermath of ISIS, have blamed the Iraqi military for labelling them as the Islamic State as well.[6]

The situation is more complicated in Syria. While ISIS is on the downturn, the landscape is riddled with smaller insurgencies and terror groups. Some are fighting for the overthrow of the Assad regime, and others are looking to set up their own proto-states that are not too dissimilar to the caliphate. Foreign powers such as Russia, the USA, Iran, and Turkey are backing their own militias, creating an extremely complicated web of violence and political interests that makes it increasingly difficult to offer a hypothesis on a plausible permanent outcome. These issues in both Iraq and Syria also leave the door open for ISIS or another similar well-orchestrated extremist entity to seep into the power vacuums being left behind.

On 18 September 2017, ISIS released an audio clip allegedly of its elusive leader, Baghdadi. The forty-six-minute clip[7] was divided into two parts. The first addressed an ideological gap in ISIS on the issue of *takfir* (or accusing another person of Islamic faith of apostasy),[8] which had garnered a lot of debate within the organization. The second was on geopolitics and ISIS, which was important amidst ISIS's losses and the prolonged silence from Baghdadi. The supposed caliph not only addressed internal ideological issues, but gave a morale boost to ISIS fighters saying territorial loss should not be linked to the 'truth' (which can be translated to the ideological goals of the organization). Baghdadi blamed the exhaustion of US foreign policy in the Middle East for its failures to counter Russia's presence in the region, and ended his speech with a Hollywood-esque statement, 'The show must go on.'[9]

Despite the losses incurred by ISIS, and the various complexities of the ground situation in both Iraq and Syria, one aspect of ISIS's influence and ability to mobilize supporters that gets lost in the narrative is the organization's reach beyond the region, and its abilities and strategies to influence individuals or groups to act in its name in foreign lands. ISIS has governorates in places such as Libya and the Philippines, among others; the Philippines is home to the Abu Sayyaf group, which is engaged in fierce fighting with the military in the besieged southern city of Marawi.[10] India has even donated a token amount to the Philippines in its battle against ISIS and its affiliates in Southeast Asia.[11]

Despite the initial euphoria, ISIS has not been able to create much of an influence in India. However, the story is not the same for other South Asian states. Afghanistan, where ISIS Khorasan Province (ISKP) has made significant inroads into the country's complex tribal districts, is now facing a new challenge of its own. Meanwhile, in Bangladesh, the ISIS-inspired attack in July 2016 in the capital Dhaka, and the ongoing Rohingya refugee crisis have raised serious concerns on the prospect of concentrated attempts at radicalization, specifically in the refugee camps, not only by ISIS, but also by Al Qaeda and a multitude of local jihadist factions. Despite the relative absence of pro-ISIS incidents in countries such as India, the threat remains active; it simply is currently muted due to local dynamics and the fact that ISIS itself has concentrated more on Europe. South Asia's complex socio-political and socio-cultural narratives remain an open door for ISIS's marketable fantasy, more than an ideology.

So far, India has had some eighty-two active cases of investigations on individuals suspected of engaging in pro-ISIS activities. These include a small group of cases that involved people travelling to or attempting to travel to Syria, Iraq,

Afghanistan, or Libya with the intention of joining ISIS, or those who have shown intentions online to do so. A handful of cases have also involved citizens' intentions to finance pro-ISIS-related activities, either in Iraq, Syria, or Afghanistan. The fact that India, with the second largest population of Muslims in the world, has only eighty-odd cases of pro-ISIS activities may be regarded as extraordinary, and a collection of hypotheses can be offered on why Indian Muslims have not taken to the idea of the caliphate's version of jihad.[12] The most significant ISIS-related case as far as Indian discourse goes was neither an attack, a bombing nor assassination, but an anonymous account on Twitter, which allegedly became one of the most vocal proponents of ISIS on the internet. The Twitter account known as ShamiWitness (@ShamiWitness) was being run by one Mehdi Masroor Biswas, an engineer in a multinational corporation in India's IT capital, Bengaluru.[13] Even during the height of his popularity as ShamiWitness, the Twitter account which even this author followed, he was not flagged by Indian authorities. He was eventually identified as the owner of the account in an investigation by British media organization Channel 4, which initially thought the account was owned by someone in Sheffield, a city in England with a sizeable South Asian population. This was widely seen as a failure of Indian agencies such as the National Technical Research Organisation (NTRO), India's premier technical intelligence agency. The other aspect highlighted from an Indian discourse, but one that was prevalent in Syria and Iraq via the demographics of many of its foreign fighters, was the fact that Biswas was a well-educated and financially stable middle-class individual whose radicalization could not be traced to traditionally accepted explanations such as poverty and lack of opportunity.

In Afghanistan and Bangladesh, the influence of ISIS has been more prominent and endangers the stability of the wider region. The July 2016 attack in an upscale restaurant in Dhaka, the Holey Artisan Bakery, where twenty-two people were killed, most of them foreigners, brought the global spotlight of terrorism to Bangladesh. The country had previously been in the news for the killings by Islamists of secular bloggers, minorities, and atheists. The 2016 attack, orchestrated by middle-class, educated Bangladeshi youth, had the signs of ISIS-inspired violence—such as using machetes to hack people to death. ISIS claimed responsibility for the attack, with its media outlets highlighting Bangladesh as its 'Bengal' governorate.[14] In a video released later, Abu Issa al-Bengali, a Bangladeshi fighter allegedly with ISIS in Syria, said, 'What you witnessed in Bangladesh . . . was a glimpse. This will repeat, repeat and repeat until you lose and we win and the sharia is established throughout the world.'[15] ISIS claiming the attack showed that local jihadist factions in the country were in touch with the Islamic State, keen to join their vision of the 'caliphate' and act upon it. The attraction towards ISIS in Bangladesh has found many takers in the country's middle class. There have been examples of Bangladeshi and Indian pro-ISIS individuals attempting to work together online to form a larger base of like-minded individuals to create an organized entity that, as other such groups have shown, would build up to an organization capable of directly co-opting with ISIS.[16] In fact, a former senior military official of Bangladesh has told this author that one of his own family members had gone to Syria to join the Islamic State, while telling them he was travelling elsewhere for leisure. This underscores the challenges in attempting to understand a person's attraction towards IS purely from a demographical, societal or cultural point of view.[17]

Meanwhile, in Afghanistan, the situation has been more complicated. ISKP, the Afghan avatar of ISIS, has more territorial presence in the vast ungoverned borderlands between Pakistan and Afghanistan along the disputed Durand Line. Most of the fighters in the ISKP brand are former Tehrik-i-Taliban Pakistan (TTP) members, who had been fleeing military operations conducted by the Pakistani armed forces in the country's tribal areas such as the Federally Administered Tribal Areas (FATA) and Waziristan. These jihadists arrived in the Achin district in the Nangarhar province and its surrounding areas under the cover of being refugees, and were initially aided by local villagers who sympathized with them for being Pashtuns.[18] These 'refugees' used the situation to look for new avenues to return to their career path of terrorism, and started to develop an environment and infrastructure for the same, possibly with backing from Pakistani military-supported actors. The USA has taken a more hands-on approach against ISKP in Afghanistan, with drone strikes and a sustained air campaign. The threat of ISKP started off as a fairly small and rudimentary group, a Taliban breakaway, however, the brand of ISIS and the organization's push to strengthen affiliates bolstered ISKP as well. To put it in further perspective, the US air campaign in the country now concentrates as much on ISKP as it does on Taliban.

Afghanistan's political vacuum and divisive socio-religious landscape could, however, become a new ground for ISIS, or the debris left behind by the so-called demise of the organization. An illustration of this is the emergence of reports on foreign ISIS fighters, including those of French and Algerian nationalities, recently arriving in Afghan districts such as Darzab in northern Jowzjan.[19] Analysts have long flagged Afghanistan as a country ripe to host the fall of the Islamic State as fighters flee Iraq and Syria, fuelled by the fact that thousands of foreign fighters in ISIS ranks were from Central Asian states that border Afghanistan in the north. For example, Jowzjan, near the city of Mazar-e-Sharif, lies only a few hundred miles from a tri-intersection of Afghanistan's borders with Turkmenistan, Uzbekistan and Tajikistan. According to the Soufan Center, 8717 foreign fighters in ISIS emerged from the erstwhile Soviet Bloc, with Turkmenistan having more than 400 fighters, Uzbekistan more than 1500, and Tajikistan 1300.[20] The hypothesis of increased terror activities in Afghanistan by the ISKP has strong empirical and historical connotations of jihadist activities in the country, for whom ISKP is only a new, globally popular brand to operate under.

The influence of ISIS in South Asia is divided according to the local politics, economics and socio-cultural complexities of each state. There is no observable pattern of convergence between various ISIS-affiliated groups or those who have claimed ownership of an attack in the name of the caliphate and only later, in an act of opportunism, has ISIS claimed their deeds. With further losses of manpower, territory and clout, ISIS has also shown signs of claiming failed attacks and rebranding them as a 'success'. As terrorism researchers Charlie Winter and Haroro J. Ingram note, singular attacks, irrespective of their size or strength, will become increasingly important for the organization as it restructures from a proto-state to a terror group, and it will take opportunities of even the most miniscule of attacks to keep the ISIS brand afloat.[21] Winter takes the example of the 'fire-bomb' attack in

London's metro train systems in September 2017 targeting a carriage at the Parsons Greens station. The attack was crude, and poorly planned and executed. The IED used was almost unbecoming of what is usually expected from ISIS attacks in Europe. The ingredients were a bucket, some wires and a failed concoction of easily available domestic chemicals. Nonetheless, ISIS claimed ownership of the attack, branded it a success, and eventually gained what it is seeking more of nowadays—a wide-reaching global narrative to counter its losses of the supposed caliphate. In more recent events, ISIS, via its news agency Amaq, claimed the killing of a security personnel in Srinagar, Jammu and Kashmir, making it its first 'official' operation in the state.[22] However, two days later, the *al-Naba* newsletter, which comes up with infographics on operational statistics for the group, did not mention India as part of the nineteen countries in which ISIS boasted of conducting attacks in 2017.

Winter and Ingram further note: 'We have to recognize that ISIS's claims of responsibility are never "just" claims of responsibility. Rather, they are central parts of the terrorist deed, psychological addendums geared toward rigging popular perceptions that are, at times, more impactful than the operation itself. Understanding how these claims—which ISIS itself describes as "media projectiles"—impact a given attack is critical if we are to weather this storm.'[23] This hypothesis sketches a picture of what ISIS's brand and influence can be translated to in regions far away from the caliphate, including in South Asia. This line of argument played out on the Sri Lanka Easter weekend attacks as well. Do we know whether ISIS was even involved? When they say 'fighters' in their claim statement, does that mean they were trained by ISIS, or is it a mere claim of their act in ISIS's name? These doubts are going to become increasingly clear with their answers.

Other analysts have used previously existing South Asian insurgency models to understand the future course of the Islamic State. In a recent study, Paul Staniland, Associate Professor of Political Science at the University of Chicago, used the final consequences of insurgencies in South Asia as a comparative to construct a hypothesis on the demise, or the final construct of Islamic State as a proto-state.[24] Staniland compares the possible future scenarios for ISIS by studying the likes of the Communist Party of India (Maoist) and United Liberation Front of Assam (ULFA) in India, Liberation Tigers of Tamil Eelam (LTTE) in Sri Lanka, and Kachin Independence Organization in Myanmar amongst others. He has devised three plausible scenarios for the future of Islamic State, the first of which is 'fighting to the death', where a comparative with the LTTE between 2006 and 2009 'Eelam War IV' was achieved.[25] The second is 'containment and possible collapse', where Staniland envisions a 'less dramatic' end to the insurgency, with 'sustained pressure' diluting the insurgency into guerilla/terror operations, an outcome which has the highest probability. Lastly, there is ISIS returning to its insurgency roots, stepping back, regrouping and reorganizing for a comeback during a more politically opportune time.[26] This is seen today particularly with the re-emergence of Taliban in Afghanistan, which during the peak of the US-led war and the relentless air-campaign in the Tora Bora mountains against Al Qaeda saw the insurgency go underground, detaching Osama bin Laden's capabilities to command Al Qaeda's various insurgencies across the Middle East.[27] Quarterly reports released by the Special Inspector

General for Afghanistan Reconstruction (SIGAR) highlights the deteriorating territorial control of the Afghan government to Taliban. According to one of the reports, Taliban increased its territorial influence to a total of 13.5 per cent of Afghan territory, fully controlling thirteen districts and influencing forty-two.[28] Ultimately, today, the USA is under negotiations with Taliban to pull out of Afghanistan after seventeen years of non-stop war, a big chunk of the $6 trillion dollar bill for the post-9/11 'war on terror' and perhaps being left red-faced for not being able to comprehensively beat a few thousand fighters with AK-47s and mountains as their frontline weapons.[29]

One anomaly that currently stands tall in ISIS's influence in South Asia is that of Pakistan. A few significant cases have come up in Pakistan; ISIS claimed responsibility for two attacks in 2017 and two in 2018. The first was in February, when an attack on a Sufi shrine in Sindh killed eighty-eight people,[30] and the second was in August, when fifteen people were killed in Quetta.[31] Both attacks were in the restive Balochistan area where Taliban's spiritual leadership—known as the Quetta Shura—also resides. But this also highlights the general internal strife between the Pakistani state and the Baloch people as well. Pakistan offers an intertwined military-jihadist-civilian complex to accurately place ISIS's presence or influence. However, in Kashmir, for both India and Pakistan-occupied Kashmir (PoK), the influence of ISIS has some quasi-official narrative. According to one of the ISIS cases being investigated in India, the accused pontificates on Kashmir. 'In my view, Kashmir was deliberately not chosen by Islamic State to launch their 'Quest for Caliphate' in al-Hind. Had it been chosen, there would have been two-front battles. First, with Indian Kuffar Army and second, with Pakistani nationalists, so-called jihadi groups Lashkar-e-Taiba (LeT), Hizbul Mujahideen, Jaish-e-Mohammed (JeM), etc. Wallahi, these factions would never accept merger with Islamic State as their foundation is based on "nationalism" or "patriotism".'[32] In simpler terms, the quagmire of India and Pakistan's overtures in Kashmir may actually help in keeping ISIS out.

The Post-ISIS Era

Over the next few months, ISIS is expected to operate more as a terror organization, closer to the operational models of Al Qaeda and its peers, as opposed to a 'caliphate'. According to some media reports, ISIS leaders have already started to move money out of Syria and Iraq in the form of secret financial transfers and business investments.[1] These resources, which to this day include ISIS earnings of over US$1 million from oil smuggling, will be critical for its future operations both in Syria, Iraq, and beyond. The internet is going to remain a steadfast access point for command and control for ISIS. Despite scholars around the world remaining divided on the magnitude of the actual threat posed online by ISIS, there is no reason to doubt that communications by the organization via Twitter, Facebook, and encrypted applications such as Telegram and Wickr, aided by its well-accustomed communications strategy using its own media ecosystem, offer continuous legitimacy to ISIS. Its online presence provides ease of access to its sympathizers and global media alike, a direct connection with its 'media jihadists', and perhaps most importantly, a continuous stream of legitimacy. To try and maintain the same level of discourse that ISIS created using media, violence, and fear during the period of 2014–15[2] would remain a critical part of its survival strategy.

The deterrence against ISIS is going to be a combination of on-ground engagement between communities and governance, along with a robust online anti-terror apparatus to keep tabs on pro-ISIS movements on social media, banking, travel, and other arenas. Many cases, for example in India, of authorities alerted towards pro-ISIS activities on Facebook came from foreign intelligence agencies and not domestic ones. While India has showcased a steadfast and robust human intelligence record against deterring terror activities, its Achilles heel remains the online world. A well-operated online intelligence network in India will not only have a domestic benefit, but also give gains to the neighbourhood with intelligence sharing, joint online operations, and database convergence to keep a check on ISIS's influence on the internet. However, an intra-South Asian combined effort on issues such as cyber-intelligence faces a massive obstacle in the form of Pakistan, which as a known state-sponsor of terror would not only be a significant loose-end in such an envisioned cyber-intelligence concert, but will look to undermine such an idea to protect its own interests.

The Attempts to Create ISIS in India

Junood-ul-Khilafa-e-Hind (JKH) was nothing; it registered nowhere, and made no dent in anyone's imagination as a feared homegrown terror group from India. The rise of the so-called Islamic State was indeed much like a fable of the promised land. Despite the fact that the geography that the insurgency retained was short-lived, its impact on the landscape of South Asia was sporadic yet present.

JKH was Shafi Armar's attempt to organize a group that would align itself with the so-called Islamic State, not online, but physically. He tried to orchestrate like-minded people from around the country to try and develop a group capable of conducting attacks in India. However, for Armar, the problem was not the lack of people showing inclination towards ISIS but the shifts that were taking place in the caliphate itself. Despite being at a peak then, 2015 onwards, ISIS was heavily involved in battles with a kaleidoscope of entities ranging from the US-led Western coalition, Russia, the Syrian Army, the Kurdish forces, Al Qaeda, and other jihadist groups, etc. By 2016, ISIS had started to be challenged in its stronghold enclaves and had started to lose its grip in parts of towns and cities it called its own.

This led to more difficulties for foreign fighters to travel to Syria to join the caliphate, forcing online recruiters such as Armar to try and convince potential recruits to not travel to Syria, but conduct operations in the name of the caliphate in their home territories. This was not necessarily the news many potential recruits wanted to hear, as they wanted to make this migration, or *hijrah*, similar to the one made by the Prophet and his followers from Mecca to Yathrib (later renamed Medina by the Prophet). The fact that this journey became difficult and was advised against by ISIS handlers themselves had an adverse effect on potential recruits—who were more interested in living in this 'ideal' Islamic ecosystem and be one of the celebrated foot soldiers—often leaving them frustrated and leading to a decline in motivation to join ISIS. However, Shafi did succeed to a certain extent in trying to orchestrate some level of cohesion amidst all those on Indian social media platforms looking to join ISIS. JKH did exist, as an entity on a very crude and simple level. Its members from similar geographies did get together and physically meet each other to discuss what next steps can be taken.

In 2015, a man named Mohamed Naser from Thanjavur, Tamil Nadu, was arrested by law enforcement agencies as part of an online surveillance programme to look at signs of radicalization in the name of ISIS. Prior to Naser as well, there had been cases of arrests for pro-ISIS activities in various parts of the country. However, the interrogations conducted in Naser's case revealed data which showcased a more organized attempt by micro-groups of pro-ISIS operatives. In this case, investigations showed that the groups were working at the behest of Armar.

Naser's footprints opened a Pandora's box, with details of meetings being held in multiple cities across the country between people who wanted to get together and discuss the ideology of the Islamic State. These meetings took place in different places including Lucknow and Deoband in Uttar Pradesh, Bengaluru and Tumakuru in Karnataka, Hyderabad and Vikarabad in Telangana, and Pune in Maharashtra. In all, this grouping had organized nine meetings for themselves to demarcate various jobs and duties.

The people involved were all in their twenties and thirties. The involvement of Armar in this attempted organization of recruits was by most accounts deep and detailed. He seemed to have kept a close eye on all the plans being discussed, and gave authoritative directions on what to do and how to go about it. The nine meetings offer an interesting window into Armar's efforts to try and group together what after all were excitable keyboard warriors into an actual terror group, capable of handling weapons, organizing recruits, cooking homegrown explosives, selecting safe training areas, safe houses and finally, committing strikes against Indian targets. During this period, Armar, going by the alias Yusuf-al-Hindi was 'Baghdadi' to these Indian groups. He made the decisions, developed strategies and was revered as the 'eahil' in this part of the world.

August 2015 was the month when JKH started some movement. The first meeting was held in the same month, with Armar's blessings, at the Devarayanadurga state forest near Tumakuru in Karnataka, a sparcely populated piece of land littered with forests and shrub areas. This was also Armar's home state; however, the selected area was more than 400 km away from his hometown of Bhatkal. It is possible that Armar was also privy to Tumakuru during past travels, and knew the land, which helped him accept recommendations for this region to be chosen for the meet.

One Syed Mujahid (also known as Abu Saad), then a thirty-two-year-old small-time businessman from Tumakuru; Mohammad Abdul Ahad, a forty-eight-year-old resident of Bengaluru; Mohammad Afzal, a thirty-three-year-old also from Bengaluru, along with one more person whose identity remains unknown, attended this first conference. The agenda was to discuss the ideology of ISIS amongst them, what they wanted to achieve, what drew them towards the group and arrangements of finances for JKH.

The second meeting for JKH was held in Deoband in Uttar Pradesh. This is significant in light of the fact that Deoband is home to the revivalist Sunni Islam movement and the often-controversial Darul Uloom Deoband Islamic seminary. The movement was founded in the late nineteenth century British India as a result of a crackdown against Mughal emperors by the British forces, and by association, Muslims in cities like Delhi were also targeted. The crackdown meant that the British took over religious sites, forcing scholars to move to other places to preserve their way of religious life, away from the revisionist and occupationist British empire. Deoband, an already thriving centre of Islamic thought and preaching, came up as one of the main alternatives and extended-neighbour to what was to become the erstwhile capital of the Mughals, Delhi.

The Darul Uloom seminary in its contemporary history has come into controversies over the Deobandi school's effects on extremist activities observed in parts of South Asia. Clerics, graduates, and members of both past and present emerging from the Deoband seminary are often observed to have ties with groups such as Taliban in Afghanistan, and other smaller groups involved in terrorism in both Pakistan and Afghanistan. While Deoband seminary itself is the nucleus of its namesake theology and its methodologies, it has come into disrepute as many Islamist groups in the region have had some sort of ties with it over the past few decades. The town itself has become synonymous with certain ideological bends, making a meeting in Deoband both symbolic and strategic from an Indian point of view. The Deoband meeting, curiously, also took place on 11 September 2015, the anniversary of the New York terror attacks. Whether this was by design or not is anyone's guess; nonetheless, it adds another possible dimension to the thinking that leads to the glorification of such ideologies.

The people attending the meet were, once again, found online. Mohammad Azhar Khan, born in 1993 and a native of Goharganj in Madhya Pradesh, Mudabbir Mushtaq Shaikh, a then thirty-three-year-old private job holder from Mumbra, Maharashtra, then nineteen-year-old Rizwan Ahmed Shaikh (aka Khalid, place of origin remains classified) and one Mehraz ur Rehman along with two others were present. The identity of the other two is contested and speculative. This meet was also organized to forward Shafi Armar's vision of what he wanted to create in India via the JKH, and took place to improve coordination efforts to create a singular umbrella over the JKH through attempting to establish leadership and ranks.

Going forward, these meetings took place in no particular design, with the third one happening in Karnataka again, in the Tumakuru Hills region, but this time the agenda was significantly different. It was Syed Mujahid once again who was taking the initiative, and leading the group towards the next step, that of assessing the physical fitness of the potential cadres, similar to a boot camp, most likely inspired by the plethora of video footage from both ISIS and Al Qaeda propaganda videos showing similar camps in remote geographies where mujahids train in warfare and physical preparedness. The attendees other than Mujahid were Abdul Ahad and Afzal, who were also present in the first meeting which took place in Tumakuru, along with three more people, one of whom is identifiable as Asif Ali, a then nineteen-year-old man from Bengaluru. The other two men were not identifiable although uncorroborated reports do suggest some names of youths from around Bengaluru itself. Along with certain physical training (more on this later in the text), the usual discussions on the development of JKH as a legitimate group and furthering the cause of the caliphate took place.

The fourth meeting took place in Bengaluru, the nerve centre of India's great story of economic rise, giving its diverse population a common purpose of development and political stability. It took place in the house of one Suhail Ahmad, a then twenty-two-year-old stone-polishing worker from Bengaluru's Mysore Road area. This meet was again mostly to discuss potential increase in recruitment and furthering the cause of *khilafat*. The fifth meeting as well, the very day after the previous one in October 2015, was held at the home of Ahmad itself. Here, moving forward from the day before, some members were assigned more specific roles to move towards a more organized structure—the insistent pressure on the narrative that the meets were largely designed to create structure. By a general assessment of the trend of why and how meetings were held up to this point, and the arguments being presented in various charge sheets, one can assume an increased pressure from Armar himself to find a person who could potentially take responsibility on the ground to rally the development of JKH.

The sixth meeting, as per accounts, perhaps showcases why Armar would have been pushing for a more structural development of the organization, as initial cracks within the groups and mismanagement started to show, also highlighting the general inadequateness of talent in the people that Armar was trying to handle remotely, mostly via the internet. This meet was held in Lucknow, the capital of Uttar Pradesh, the second meet in the state after Deoband. The Lucknow gathering was organized by one Mohammed Aleem, a then twenty-three-year-old resident of Indiranagar, Lucknow. It took place at Aleem's uncle's house and was attended by one Mohammed Nafees Khan from Hyderabad, Mudabbir Shaikh and Mohammed Hussain Khan from Mumbai, Rizwan Ahmed, and two others. Mohammad Azhar Khan, from Madhya Pradesh, arrived at this meet with two other unknown people who were willing to join ISIS and JKH. The group turned away the two unknowns and did not allow them to participate. Moving forward, the seventh meet was held in Hyderabad at the house of one Mohammed Shareef Moinuddin Khan, a then fifty-eight-year-old resident of Nizam Colony, Hyderabad. The crux of this meet, attended by Syed Mujahid who had organized the Tumakuru meets and others, was to discuss the hijrah to Syria, or the holy journey to the caliphate.

The final meet, in this particular series, was held in Pune, Maharashtra, two months later in December. This meet saw Abu Anas from Jaipur, Nafees Khan and three other people, along with one of their wives also in attendance. Curiously, one of the main points of discussion here was the development of a personalized JKH app for communications between recruits and members of the intended group. This, again, has footprints of thinking that may have come directly from Armar. However, this was also the time when there was a lot of public scrutiny against social media platforms such as Facebook and Twitter to crackdown on pro-ISIS accounts globally, which in turn forced a lot of such chatter to other platforms that offered end-to-end encryption. Most of the chatter moved to Telegram, while other lesser-known platforms were also used for the same. The fact that this was being thought of, but asked to be debated amongst people who were, at best, of average intellectual calibre showcases the seeds of failure right at the onset of JKH.

Not all was going as planned for Armar. During the end course of these meetings, and on one of the voice calls he made using Skype, Armar was informed unceremoniously that the group had self-appointed an 'emir' for all India operations, Mohammad Azhar Khan, who was all of twenty-three years old at that time. Rizwan Ahmed, who had been keeping a direct line of communication with Armar, told the meeting that he would need to confirm this with him. Upon being informed of the same, Armar told Rizwan to put him on speakerphone so as to address the gathering, and an infuriated Armar lashed out at the group. He let them know of his displeasure in stern language and tone, and that Khan was not senior enough to take up the job, a job whose appointment would be done by him, and not via any democratic process within the group.

Armar appointed Mudabbir Shaikh from Maharashtra as 'Emir-e-Hind'. Despite the disjointedness of JKH, this was a significant moment, even if only for symbolism, that the man trying to handle most pro-ISIS operations in India appointed an emir for operations here. Along with the Emir, Khan, the one designated by others as Emir was instead given the tag of 'Askari

Emir' (or in charge of the military operations) and Mohammed Nafees Khan became the 'Maliyat Emir' (in charge of money and finance). Meanwhile, interestingly, Armar tells the group that another man, whom he seems to have pre-selected, but who lives outside India, will be coming in to take over the responsibility of 'Media Emir', to take care of communications of the JKH. The identity of the person in question remains unknown, however the importance of the 'Media Emir' person cannot be undersold as it would hold prominence in creating propaganda material to further recruitment activities. Parallel to this period in 2015, ISIS was creating a storm the world over with the reach of its own propaganda videos, magazines, newsletters and use of social media platforms to recruit, dispense information, and use this technology to beam themselves into the living rooms of every corner on the planet.

However, the above hierarchical architecture for the JKH was not immediately acceptable to everyone involved. Despite Armar's position at the top of the command structure of the group, there were disagreements over the positions decided by him for the emirs. With the disagreements seemingly continuing, however, the group eventually dispersed with the initially appointed emirs continuing their newly found positions. The initial mandate was, as mentioned previously, to get safe communications arranged.

The group, led by Emir Mudabbir who had returned to Mumbai, started to accumulate the required tools. Smartphones and laptops were purchased for some of the people to initiate better contact with each other. This included, initially, buying more than ten SIM cards which were procured allegedly without any documentation provided from an Aircel outlet owned by a man named Imran in Hyderabad's Toli Chowki area. There lies no evidence of whether the shop owner was just a bystander, unaware of the plots, or a distant enabler who looked the other way when documentation was required. It is also important to highlight, in general, the lax regulatory systems when it comes to the identification necessary to get SIM cards for phones and the possibilities of gaming the system to get 'loose' SIM cards.

Another meeting was now planned to take place in Bengaluru, with Mohammed Nafees Khan travelling to the city from Dadar in Mumbai where in another meet, this time at the home of Asif Ali, pseudonyms (or kunniyat in Arabic), similar to Armar's Yusuf-al-Hindi moniker, were handed out. Asif, the host, undertook the identity of Armansani, Abdul Ahad became Abu Ali, and so on. Copies of ISIS-produced texts were also distributed to further strengthen their resolve towards the caliphate.

This meeting also saw an increased role for Mohammed Nafees. Seeing disagreements over positions and so on, Armar seemingly distributed power in order to make sure people were happy and there was no major internal wrangling over positions and so on. From a quick glance of all the above involved so far, one takeaway that can be observed is that members who were young, around twenty years old, were more assertive in their bargaining for power and position than some of the older members. Nafees started to be the 'handler' of most JKH activities occurring in southern India, and in the same month of December 2015, on Christmas day, another meeting took place where he convened the group to take a pledge in the name of JKH, which when read, also asserted his own micro-command beyond that of both Armar and Mudabbir.

'We should all adhere to the exact terms and conditions that will be discussed in the meeting, and we need to show our complete obedience to these terms. Allah be our witness,' the oath roughly read. Nonetheless, there was internal dissent, as Abdul Ahad and Afzal, the former given responsibilities of media, did not abide by the mandates handed over to them. Nonetheless, the processes moved on. There are very few details on what these internal strifes and disagreements over responsibilities and titles led to, but presumably as Armar was seen as 'Emir of JKH' one can guess that ultimately he made the calls and distributed titles in a manner which would allow all involved to keep working within JKH's disjointed framework.

By January 2016, things moved beyond the organization stage as Armar asked Nafees to start looking for places to set up training camps and make hideouts. Nafees, along with some others from the group, did recces of neighbouring regions of Hyderabad such as Vikarabad, 75 km outside the city with vast open farmland and wasteland alike. Mohammed Shareef Moinuddin, the eldest of the lot, took Nafees, Abu Anas and three others to a vacant farmhouse in the region, which he said belonged to a friend of his and could be used as one of the first training camps of the JKH. The group then also visited a nearby lake where they tested their endurance and fitness by kayaking.

Nafees, responsible for money, also was tasked to collect materials to try and make IEDs to be used in terror strikes. During this trip to Hyderabad, Nafees also visited the Narsapur forest area carrying a pipe bomb, a crude IED he had made at home. The trip to the forest was to find a suitable and empty space to actually test it out without raising alarm. However, thanks to India's robust population of more than 1.3 billion citizens, Nafees was unable to find a suitable location and the intended test did not happen.

Nafees abandoned his immediate plan to test the IED, and boarded a train, leaving Hyderabad behind and headed towards West Bengal, where he met another unknown person in Durgapur, about 170 km north of the capital Kolkata, and then onwards to Burdwan where he met one Ashik Ahmmed. Nafees handed over a smartphone to Ahmmed with the necessary apps so that he could communicate safely with them and others. Armar had told Nafees precisely what he had to do on this trip, and that was, to scout for weapons.

During one of the conversations in the region, initiated with people that Ahmmed knew, someone said that they knew a mason who lived near the Indian border with Bangladesh, a popular gunrunning area, who could get some weapons. The mason informed Nafees and Ahmmed that weapons were not a problem, and if they wanted, he could get them guns such as the AK-47 rifle as well, a weapon of choice for terrorists, insurgents and states alike. Knowing that weapons would be available for purchase in the region, Nafees announced that he intended to build a base camp in the area for future activities. During these discussions, he also addressed an unknown number of people, explaining to them what ISIS stood for and what they intended to build in India as part of the caliphate. Oddly, he also discussed how jihadists had killed the judge who had sentenced erstwhile Iraqi dictator Saddam to death, a piece of fake news that has been circulated over social media on and off since 2014.[1] This was 2016, and why, how, and to what end this particular information was used as a tool to instigate the listeners to join ISIS remains unknown. This could just be exploiting the ignorance of these people living in a remote part of the state of West Bengal or just an example to showcase how high profile their activities have become, so as to make recruitment more attractive.

Meanwhile, Armar had also told Mudabbir Shaikh to start working on procurement of weapons. Mudabbir's position as 'Emir-e-Hind' by this time was convoluted; however, information available does show Armar's trust in Mudabbir to handle recruits, people and funds all at the same time was high. Mudabbir, born in 1982, was nineteen years old when 9/11 happened. The ensuing blowback against Muslims that was witnessed not just in the USA but around the world in some shape or form affected Mudabbir. The fact that the word 'terrorist' was being attached with Muslims across the world angered him, and after the New York terror attack, he felt as if he was being treated like a second-class citizen and was disenchanted with the general place of Muslims in the world. To fight back, he decided to head down the path of jihad.

This was 2007, when Facebook was still a predominantly US phenomenon and Twitter was just a few months old. Nonetheless, social media was taking off with other products and brands taking over the market. During this period, social media site Orkut, founded in 2004, was gaining ground in India, specifically amongst the youth. It was on this, now defunct, social media platform—where at that time most took the 'social' part literally and used it as innocently as it was conceptualized—that Mudabbir found accounts of persons who were fighting against the Americans in Afghanistan. The account Mudabbir contacted, called Mujahid Fi Sabiullah, interestingly as per information available knew exactly where to send Mudabbir to further his intent of joining jihad. The account's owner(s) told Mudabbir to contact him via the Jamat-e-Islami Hind, via their offices in Mumbai's Byculla area. Mudabbir attended a host of events and programmes there, which added significantly to his thought process of taking up jihad.

Mudabbir came in touch with Armar via his Yusuf-al-Hindi pseudonym on Facebook in 2013, when Mudabbir searched for pages talking about khilafat and the agendas to fight for it. On one of these pages Mudabbir started to debate over khilafat with other users, and attracted the attention of Armar who was on the lookout for recruits in India. He directly messaged Mudabbir on Facebook and introduced himself as a member of the Ansar-ul-Tawhid (AuT) fighting in Afghanistan. Armar then set up a Skype account for Mudabbir for them to have an audio conversation (interesting to note here that Skype in 2013 had very basic encryption, and only got end-to-end encryption in 2018). While Mudabbir and Armar connected on and off over the months, this became a pivotal time for Armar himself as well. During a conversation with Mudabbir in the summer of 2014, a year after both of them got in touch with each other, Armar informed Mudabbir that he had now become a follower of ISIS chief Baghdadi, having taken *bayat* in his name, and was to move to Syria to join ISIS directly. Between this conversation and the next, three months passed, during which Armar successfully shifted from Afghanistan to Syria. During another Skype call, he informed Mudabbir that he had suggested his name as a nominee to take bayat in the name of Baghdadi and ISIS.

This sold well with Mudabbir, who, by way of knowing Armar since 2013, had started to build confidence in him that he could be one of the main propagators of ISIS in India. Armar in the meantime started work on two fronts, transfer of funds for JKH to conduct meetings, which would lead to conducting of terror strikes on Indian targets, and giving basic instructions on how to make IEDs from everyday materials. Armar himself by this time would have been fairly experienced with having served in the Afghan theatre for a while. IEDs are commonly used in the Afghan war, and universally are the preferred means of attack of militant groups.

He started to teach Mudabbir how to make IED timers using a mobile phone, highlighting that this method has been very useful against US forces in Afghanistan. To put some perspective to this—in 2010, IED attacks in Afghanistan wounded more than 3500 US soldiers. More than 600 soldiers died in battle in the same year, out of which around 360 were killed by IEDs. The same year, in total, more than 14,000 IEDs were found deployed in the Afghan theatre. Based on such data, it is safe to believe that Armar and the AuT were well versed in the manufacturing of IEDs and wanted to pass on the knowledge to recruits in India.

Understanding IEDs is an important aspect of understanding this version of modern terror propagated by ISIS. IEDs have been part of insurgency warfare for a long period of time due to the common availability of ingredients used to make these explosive devices, ranging from fertilizers to batteries. In December 2018, Indian agencies conducted raids in Delhi and Uttar Pradesh against alleged pro-ISIS cells planning to attack targets in the country. The police recovered locally made guns, bullets, printouts of ISIS-related imagery, and firecrackers, which caused amusement amongst people as to why such a feared organization was supposedly using firecrackers.

These raids were also important to show that since ISIS was seen as a terror group active mostly in Syria by this point of time, general understanding and discourse on the same was fairly pedestrian. In fact, the firecrackers are capable of being an integral part of lethal IEDs, and instructions on how to go about making these are available online fairly easily, with various terror groups, such as Al Qaeda, posting bomb-making instructions online predating ISIS as a group itself.

In fact, IEDs remain one of the most lethal and effective tool of terrorism globally. Since IEDs use components, which are of daily industrial and commercial use, it is extremely difficult to control and track shipments of the same that may be used for terrorism. Shell companies, the black market and increasing difficulties in trying to stop the flow of money due to increased globalization and technological advancements make it all that easier for IEDs to become a potent weapon.

To illustrate this further, Indian companies were found to have a footprint in the IEDs that were used by ISIS in Syria. That these IEDs were going to end up in a feared terror group's hands was unknown to these companies. According to an extensive report by Conflict Armament Research (CAR) published in 2016, detonating cords, detonators, safety fuses and mobile phones used to set the timers on IEDs manufactured in India were also found at the scene of IED attacks in Syria. Products of seven Indian companies including Rajasthan Explosives and Chemicals, Chamundi Explosives, Nokia Solutions and Networks India, and Solar Industries, which were found to be components of these weapons, were in some probability not intended to be used for these purposes as they were shipped to buyers in Turkey and Lebanon under government-issued licenses from India.[2] There remains a possibility of these kind of components also being imported by ISIS via its own infrastructure, operating shell, or fake companies in order to ship these to third countries before making their way across to Syria. Both Turkey and Lebanon share large swathes of border with Syria.

Along with mobile phones, Armar also tried to teach Mudabbir, via Skype, how to make IEDs using matchstick powder, which is a concoction of everyday materials such as sulphur, starch, glue and potassium chlorate. All easily available over-the-counter from shops. The plan was to make pipe bombs using the powder, set off by a mobile phone timer. Mudabbir also used the internet to find bomb-making instructions, something that is available in plenty, just a Google search away.

Again, like Nafees, Mudabbir was also to handle a chunk of finances. This history between Mudabbir and Armar is why, as discussed earlier, the latter wanted him to be 'Emir of ISIS's India operations'. The fact that Armar seemingly had 'nominated' Mudabbir within the ISIS hierarchies, gave him credibility to handle more important organizational things, such as money. While it remains unknown as to who handled Armar within ISIS while he tried to build something in India, such a nomination would build confidence within the ISIS infrastructure that Armar was dealing with safe and committed people.

Armar sent funds to Mudabbir via hawala channels—an alternative way of transferring money without conducting bank transfers using a network of trusted hawala brokers—while also raising funds domestically. Mudabbir himself offered *zakat* (zakat in Islam means donating a portion of your earnings as a religious obligation that could also be seen as tax. It is seen as a religious obligation of all Muslims) to Armar in support of the cause of khilafat. Earlier, Armar had also made an account for Mudabbir on encrypted messaging app Trillian. Through their chats, Armar managed to transfer Rs 1,06,000 to Mudabbir, which was delivered to him via a third person, a shop owner who ran a small textiles business in Mumbai's Dongri suburb. Once this was received, Mudabbir sent a confirmation message to Armar via the same Trillian ID that Armar had made for him. A second transfer via hawala systems was made, this time for

Rs 4,80,000, to further ISIS activities, delivered this time by another man from Zaveri Bazaar, Mumbai, who handed over the cash to Mudabbir on a roadside. This method of moving funds highlighted two important points on financing terrorism in India. First, that despite the decades-long scrutiny on hawala channels in moving money, it showcases that unregulated financial highways still exist and options to game the system, albeit difficult, are not impossible. Second, that Armar was clearly capable of using the pre-existing goodwill and ecosystem of the erstwhile Indian Mujahideen (IM) to finance his ISIS-in-waiting group that Indian agencies were recognizing as IM trying to resurface as ISIS, a better, globally-recognized brand title. The delivery system to Mudabbir seems to be existing infrastructure that may have gone underground amidst the crackdown against IM but was never dismantled, and had been revived by Armar in parts.

Mudabbir was now instructed to distribute these funds in parts to a number of people that Armar was handling, both the ones mentioned above and others as well. Majority of this money was for travel expenses while attending or orchestrating recruitment meetings, to purchase smartphones for easier communications, and to help get easier access to the internet and communication tools.

Armar by this time had a wide network of people he was in contact with, going well beyond the few highlighted here. By this time, he had started introducing these contacts to each other, weaving together a network moving from online to offline.

'The ISIS Pool'

It is theorized that the period of transition of an individual from thinking about radicalization to acting upon it is perhaps the only time when law enforcement can act as an intervention to stop an impending act of terror. The advent of technology, the internet and ease of global communication has also made it easier for potential recruits to get in touch with like-minded individuals with relative ease. As ISIS was growing in geography in both Syria and Iraq, individuals who identified with the idea of khilafat looked for each other online to discuss the ideology and mostly plan their respective travels to the Islamic State.

Due to the fact that social media platforms were slow to respond to their products being used to further jihadist causes, a lot of the initial attempts to collect online for this went unchecked, and the few 'security' systems the platforms had to fight against basic threats were easy to game via multiple IDs and false accounts.

Many cases in India, in fact, most, under investigation are of people propagating ISIS ideology, and not necessarily moving across borders to try and join the caliphate. However, there is another side to this discourse, that of Indians not just looking to join ISIS but Indians becoming one of the premier online recruiters for ISIS itself.

As a journalist, with most of my bandwidth concentrated towards following the developments in Iraq and Syria, South Asia was an interesting 'failure' for ISIS as despite the number of Muslims residing in the region, no major organisation of ISIS was formed in the region other than Afghanistan. This was, sort of, a watershed moment for those who covered terrorism, specifically that from a global perspective and not just the Pakistan theatre. It is rare to witness the rise of a terror group with the amount of gusto that ISIS came up with, making it on global front-pages within months of its existence as the 'Islamic State' and using the internet like no other before to digitally command and conquer.

Getting access to these online groups of ISIS sympathizers became a sort of race amongst journalists themselves during the rise of ISIS. Who would cover this new terror group, seemingly the most heinous in the world, willing to talk to the press, marketing itself and revelling in the spotlight being offered by the world as they murdered, decapitated, raped, and burned citizens of both Iraq and Syria? In one of the online pro-ISIS groups I managed to enter earlier, with the help of another journalist who got in thanks to an articulate and internet-savvy ISIS sympathizer from Europe. Many journalists and researchers alike were getting access to these groups, as a proper crackdown by social media platforms against these ecosystems was yet a few years away. In fact, it was in 2013 when one could say the first proper use of social media for an act of terror took place when the group Al Shabaab, an Al Qaeda-aligned outfit operating in eastern Africa, live-tweeted an attack by its members on the upscale Westgate Mall in the Kenyan capital of Nairobi. The minimal success of the attacks in Kenya was the seed planted for a rabid ecosystem to come out, transferring from platform to platform, using the very concept of the internet in their favour to exist in the digital world, with the world able to do little about it.

Journalists used to act as 'lurkers' in these pro-ISIS groups. The one I was part of on Telegram was fairly quiet in the beginning. While it was Twitter that saw the first few instances of jihadist handles operating freely on apps meant to bring the world closer, it was Telegram and its offering of end-to-end encryption and features such as temporary links that gave the pro-ISIS online ecosystem a suitable home for the long run. It was on Telegram that us lurkers, using fake names and IDs, and phones and mobile numbers, quietly entered these groups and tried to look a part of this new quagmire of digital jihadists to not just understand what was happening, but also look for clues on who these people were, what they wanted, where they were from and why these tech-savvy, educated Muslims had found such affinity for ISIS. As mentioned, in many cases, the group members knew who the lurkers were. Some found our presence acceptable, while others didn't. Getting kicked out of these groups was a common occurrence, and existing in these online spaces was an art form in itself. Every now and then, one had to participate, sharing links to propaganda or saying something familiar so as to not raise any suspicion. However, post-2017 when surveillance against online identities really tightened up, lurkers lost their spots in such groups as they attempted to hide from the ire of law enforcement agencies. I was also kicked out of the two main pro-ISIS groups I was lurking in for months, one in 2017 and then my last one in mid-2018. No warnings were given to my user account on why I was being shown the door, but it was no surprise that the people running these channels on Telegram were fine with me as a lurker, and had a fairly good idea that I was either a researcher or a journalist. However, in a fast tightening environment, they perhaps couldn't take a chance.

During this period of the rise of the internet as a terror propagator, one account on Twitter particularly caught everyone's eyes. The account went by the handle @ ShamiWitness, and was openly not just propagating the rise of ISIS, but talking to potential recruits to join the group and advising them on how to travel to either Iraq or Syria. This account was oddly open about its views, and no one at first was sure whether it was a 'him', a 'her', or a bunch of people running it for ISIS. Whether they were actually in Iraq, Syria or somewhere in the Middle East was anyone's guess; nonetheless, ShamiWitness was responsive to everyone. This didn't mean he was only forthcoming to pro-ISIS people; his exchanges on Twitter's direct messages included everyone from researchers to journalists and scholars. In fact, ShamiWitness played it smart (or stupid, both are arguable), and did a lot of work in the open. He amassed nearly 40,000 followers, including this author, who were watching him propagate and talk to pro-ISIS Twitter users. He had more than 1,24,000 tweets, and was carefree in the distribution of information from behind his anonymous identity. This Twitter profile was straightforward; his display picture was a juxtaposed image of a Muslim man and a lion. His Twitter bio said, 'Bilad ash Sham, Sunni Revolutions, Economic Collapse, Post-industrial society, Technology, History, etc. RTs not endorsement. Following not endorsement'. His cover image said 'Shami Witness' in big, block letters on a black and white background. He had a link to a Blogspot site as 'ShamiWitness' itself and his Twitter joining date on his page was stated as July 2009. So, the possibility that this account was operated under a different name, or had completely different motives of being on Twitter prior to the rise of ISIS is high. However, in 2013–14, the lax approach towards cyber security and counterterrorism online gave ShamiWitness immense access to both pro-ISIS folks and others alike, who were curious to travel to the caliphate. It is interesting to note here that ShamiWitness was more of a 'pop-culture' jihad propagator, while out of his 1,24,000 odd tweets, nearly 1,22,000 were pro-ISIS messages, both interacting with others on the platform with similar inclinations and advising them on how to travel to the caliphate. The advisories that ShamiWitness gave seemed to be quite well informed. While his Twitter feed was taken off and all the data seized (not permanently deleted, but deleted off the Twitter platform), some examples of his interactions remain as part of news reports from that year. Questions asked on Twitter had an impressive response time, mostly within minutes, for those looking for advice on how to cross over into Iraq and Turkey.

The below excerpt from ShamiWitness's Twitter feed is from June 2014:

> At 12.31 a.m. on 24 June (2014), Twitter handle @ TalabAlHaqq tweeted to ShamiWitness with two other handles also tagged in, saying: 'Salam akhi (akhi translating to 'my brother' in Arabic), how can a mihajir stuck in southeastern Turkey get help crossing through to Raqqa insha allah??'
>
> Within seventeen minutes of the tweet, ShamiWitness replied: '@TalabAlHaqq: walayakum salam. Tal Abyad

crossing open now @AbuUmar8246, @onthatpath3, and @ TalabAlHaqq in Jerabulus (Syrian town near Aleppo) also.'[1]

During the same time, in the UK, law enforcement became curious on who ShamiWitness was and who ran this account. According to some sources, this curiosity emerged from the intelligence that the account could have been run by someone of South Asian descent living on the outskirts of London. However, the search for this person in the UK went cold, but not before finding out who it was and from where this man operated.

On 11 December 2014, British news network Channel 4 ran a segment on ShamiWitness, outing him as one 'Mehdi', later coming to be known as Mehdi Masroor Biswas, a then twenty-four-year-old educated professional working in India's technology hub Bengaluru. The relatively famous ShamiWitness not only lost his anonymous fame, but oddly, for Channel 4, even gave an interview, as 'Mehdi', a relatively calm young man answering the journalists' questions about who he was and why he did what he was doing with this Twitter account. Mehdi announced that if he had his way, he would also have travelled 'to ISIS' and joined the group. 'If I had a chance to leave everything and join them, I might have,' he told the journalists. Upon being asked what stopped him from doing so, he said, what could perhaps be described as a very South Asian trait, or just plainly as bad characteristics for a successful jihadist, that his family needed him in India. 'My parents; they are basically dependent on me.' Pushing the questioning further, after getting a positive answer once again that he would have 'probably' joined ISIS, Mehdi was asked whether he believed in the methods of the Islamic State, those of beheadings, executions and so on. Continuing with his calm answers, with a hint of quiver, he replies, 'Beheadings are discussed in the Quran and Hadith itself. I don't think any honest Muslim will ever tell you that he's against beheadings per se.'

'Are you an honest Muslim, then?' the Channel 4 journalist asks.

'I try to, but I am not sure if I am,' Mehdi says, with a slight sense of grief, and perhaps acceptance of fate, that it was the end of the road for ShamiWitness and his social media 'fame'.

Expectedly, Mehdi tried to hide the fact that he encouraged people online to move to the 'caliphate'. 'Just because somebody follows me that doesn't mean I am the reason for their moving to ISIS,' he said. 'There are real reasons why people get "radicalized".'

After the interview, Mehdi told *Channel 4* that he was going to shut down his Twitter alter ego.

The general un-impressiveness of Mehdi in real life as a person compared to his alpha-jihadist presence online was perhaps a norm. The fact that he could not leave to join ISIS because of family doesn't bode well for the very persona he had built for himself online. A family man, with dependent parents, working as an executive in the swarm of India's IT hub while also being a savvy online jihadist on the side was always going to have a short shelf life.

But the boons provided by ShamiWitness were not only for pro-ISIS people around the world. Researchers and journalists had access to him as well, through direct messages, or even, openly. This author as well got two replies during that period of time after probing him in an attempt to quantify the kind of interest he was witnessing from people within India willing or looking to join the Islamic State in Syria or Iraq (unfortunately, in 2014, the replies to the queries were not documented by the author).

However, other scholars such as Hassan Hassan, a research fellow at the Tahrir Institute for Middle East Policy (TIMEP), director of the Non-state Actors in Fragile Environments programme at the Center for Global Policy in Washington D.C. and co-author of *ISIS: Inside the Army of Terror,* had a closer brush with Mehdi just a day before the Channel 4 revelations came out. 'Will you journalists ever talk about the continuous deportation of Arabs, burning their homes and properties . . . and killing them by YPG [Syrian Kurdish militants]? Or are you waiting for Hasaka (a province in northern Syria) to be Arab-free before the faux wailing can begin? Aren't they Syrians too or is YPG that much venerated that their war crimes can't be touched.' This was a direct message by ShamiWitness to Hassan, a day before.[2]

This, of course, raises the question whether the entire Channel 4 unmasking of ShamiWitness literally unfolded over a twenty-four-hour period or whether he was aware that journalists were on to his identity from before but kept a calm face in front of such an eventuality. However, as Hassan notes in his *Foreign Policy* piece about Mehdi, the fact did remain that ShamiWitness was indeed one of the most accurate dispenser of ISIS and the Syrian jihadist landscape, with seemingly good understanding of ground dynamics, intra-group relations, and local grievances of populations and people living in these territories.

'The real problem with Mehdi was not reliability,' Hassan wrote further. 'For professionals who followed him because he echoed the voices of jihadists, it was not propaganda either—we knew he was a propagandist for the Islamic State and treated his arguments and information accordingly. What was truly troubling about Mehdi is that he represented a certain category of Islamic State sympathizer across the Muslim world—those who wholeheartedly back the group in public even though they do not share the same characteristics of the jihadists they purportedly support.'

This argument is perhaps magnified by the previously highlighted fact that Mehdi could not travel to the caliphate due to his family obligations. In an ideal 'jihadist' mindset, such an excuse could make his resolve towards the cause questionable, as most foreign recruits of ISIS made it to Syria or Iraq by abandoning all sense of family and purpose, finding greater purpose in this well-marketed 'holy war' for the ancient land. Nonetheless, Mehdi's astuteness in his online world was perhaps seen as a boon by ISIS hierarchies as well, who may have fed him information and pushed him to propagate their line further in order to attract foreign fighters, for many of whom he may well have been the starting point of their vision to join and live in the caliphate.

However, amidst all this, perhaps the greatest oddity was that ShamiWitness operated for more than a year as this persona in Bengaluru, the 'cyber-city' of India and home to the country's 'IT revolution'. The fact that he managed to go unspotted by the country's law enforcement for this long is the biggest loophole to be highlighted. It is well understood that India's counterterrorism capacities online are limited in nature, and the agencies responsible for the same move at traditional bureaucratic speeds to counter these threats while the threats themselves manage to remain a fair few steps ahead of the online policing curve. Indian agencies only sprung into action once Mehdi's identity went public. Prior to this, while Channel 4 had the said information in its possession and was building the story, Indian spooks remained clueless about the operations of ShamiWitness.

The lethargy behind these events from India's perspective is a grave cause for concern and exposes deep gaps in modern counterterrorism thinking. Despite the effective use of the internet by ISIS, India's counter-narrative and counterterrorism measures online to date are archaic at best, lacking the sense of urgency to recognize the online space as a major scene of criminal activities. This is despite the fact that India placed additional measures from 2014 at airports across the country to keep an extra eye on single males travelling to the Middle East. New Delhi worked with its partner countries in West Asia to flag any individuals that may have been highlighted for proscribing.

To illustrate these policy gaps, ISIS once again provides a case in point.

The Online Six Degrees of Separation

The online sphere, as discussed before, is critical to ISIS and even more so now with the loss of its caliphate. The media output is considered as a sacrosanct feature of ISIS's operations, giving it the same importance as its militias fighting the physical battles in the real world. ISIS has used Twitter, Facebook, WhatsApp and, perhaps most importantly, Telegram, to great effect in both spreading its ideology and recruiting. To understand the success of ISIS's outreach using new media platforms, it is first important to answer how it props up its online armies to execute so-called 'media jihad', offering its intended audience stage-managed, well executed and produced content glorifying the caliphate and its conquests. The recognition of media as a tool goes beyond social media to forums, old-school chat rooms and even cassettes to deliver sermons by preachers. Osama bin Laden was himself well aware of the power of television, seeing its effects in action during the first Gulf War, and cable television. September 11 was a 'televised' terror strike, which knew the power of media, imagery and so on. It was televised then, and today it can be replayed by anyone on YouTube. It's a permanent fixture of Al Qaeda's magnum opus against the West.

Abu Musab al-Suri, a suspected Al Qaeda member and jihadi writer born in Syria but of Spanish citizenship currently known to be in a Syrian prison after his deportation from Pakistan in 2005, also put forward the internet as an oppurtunity. In his seminal work published in 2004 titled *A Call to a Global Islamic Resistance*, Suri highlighted the use of the internet for jihadists, so much so that he prophesized that due to technological advancements in media tools, physical hierarchical structures were no longer needed for conducting jihad, and new media would be sufficient. He ideated that every Muslim's home can become a training camp or forward base, rather than relying on large fifty-two bases that could be easily targeted by their enemies.

In understanding ISIS's media strategy, a key document is *Media Operative, You Are a Mujahid, Too*—a guide to the group's ideas, thoughts, requirements and propaganda. This text is derived from a shorter version on media ethics for ISIS published by the Al-Himma Library, a media outlet tasked with publishing mostly religious pamphlets and manifestos for ISIS. Released in April 2016 in Arabic on Telegram, the document was written by an anonymous author(s) and addresses ISIS's online support base. It called the individual supporters of the group and the caliphate online, around the world, as the 'media mujahidin'. The document's job is seemingly to make sure that the online support base does not feel any less important than the ground troops constituting the physical caliphate; this highlights the importance of the media narrative for ISIS. One of the more pertinent sections of this document states that the media is a battleground as well, and its importance should not be undermined. While the messaging here seems to highlight the importance of the media wars for ISIS, the background of this particular take on the importance of information warfare is clouded and based on false information itself—in other words, propaganda within propaganda. According to scholar Charlie Winter, the above messaging was in fact first delivered by Al Qaeda's Zawahiri in a letter to Zarqawi, highlighting AQI's brutal approach to jihad and explaining that such 'ultraviolent' approach was a bad way to promote their ideology—it displayed them in poor light in the media to local populations of the region. However, ISIS, already at odds with Al Qaeda's leadership, turned this approach on its head and formalized their approach via propaganda for their media mujahids.

Amaq News Agency, an outlet that regularly releases ISIS statements, operational details including infographics, and runs media outputs on platforms such as Telegram using official groups is at the forefront of this propaganda programme. There is also Rumiyah, a glossy magazine brought out under the 'Himmah Publications' badge, which may be called 'the Newsweek' of Islamic State, that covers pro-ISIS activities from around the world. For example, Rumiyah's issue number ten's cover story, 'The Jihad in East Asia', describes the Philippines's war against the Abu Sayyaf group (unofficially known as Islamic State of Iraq and the Levant—the Philippines Province) after the Islamist group announced its allegiance to Baghdadi in 2016.

The third outlet, *Dabiq*, is now defunct and the former avatar of Rumiyah. It was *Dabiq* that initially brought to mainstream discussion ISIS's capabilities for formalizing information delivery. It had a glossy look and well-produced layouts, and seemed like a professional, state-run media enterprise. According to analysts such as Harleen K. Gambhir, *Dabiq* was a representation of

(Issue no. 10 of ISIS's *Rumiyah* magazine)[1]

an outward-looking interpretation of ISIS, working towards becoming influential beyond the borders of territorial gains in Iraq and Syria. The magazine was discontinued and replaced with *Rumiyah*, after the group lost the prophesized town of Dabiq near Aleppo, where ISIS sought the biggest battle between good and evil, to Syrian rebels in October 2016.

Equating online supporters to ground fighters of the caliphate was important for ISIS's strategy to succeed. They needed the online ecosystem to create patches of influence across the world, which could then be honed into conducting attacks or simply keeping their supporters motivated enough to back the idea of the Islamic State unquestionably. To illustrate this further, let us take the case of one Mohammed Sirajuddin, an Indian citizen who in 2015 was found in the grasp of ISIS's online propaganda machinery.

Sirajuddin, a resident of Gulburga in Karnataka, was arrested by police in December 2015 in Jaipur, Rajasthan, for his alleged pro-ISIS activities on the internet. Sirajuddin, then in his early thirties, was accused of using online media platforms such as Facebook, WhatsApp, Telegram and so on to incite and recruit pro-ISIS people to perform the holy trip to the caliphate.

Sirajuddin, who at the time was living in the Jawahar Nagar locality of the city, allegedly ran a number of social media accounts and groups to propagate ISIS ideology. There have been multiple instances of such groups with both Indian and international members, often with no connections between each other than their affinity for Islamic State, coming up across the board on multiple platforms. Sirajuddin was seemingly one of the people tightly woven into the pro-ISIS narrative.

He created multiple online identities, Facebook groups, Telegram groups and e-mail IDs in late 2015 in an attempt to bring together like-minded people. His Facebook activities and promotions got him in touch with a host of allegedly pro-ISIS individuals from around the world. He shared links to his Telegram group called Official Bug, which claimed to have active Islamic State members from Libya. This almost became a selling point for the chat group, and Sirajuddin befriended many people online from around the world who shared his views and affinity towards ISIS. Geography was not a strategic play here; the group was not created to help local radicalized and pro-ISIS people in a particular locality, or even India as a country, but just as an avenue to gather ISIS sympathizers from the world over. As far as radicalization online goes, once again, Sirajuddin's case highlights the ideological confusion, or a complete lack of ideological understanding of jihadist groups and their mandates. Sirajuddin, like others, blurred the lines between Al Qaeda and ISIS related groups.

During his online activities, Sirajuddin also came in touch with women who were inclined towards joining the caliphate. In one instance, he started to converse with a Kenyan national who had the online identity Ukhty Minaa. During discussions with other fellow members of his Official Bug group on Telegram, he professed his desire to marry Minaa. Upon being reminded that he is a married man, Sirajuddin allegedly replied: 'Marrying a Mujahidah (a woman mujahid) is a dream. Inshallah she will be my ticket to jannah.'

The talks between the members of these online groups, while fable-like in nature, seem to factor in the eventualities of their capture or arrest due to these communications and not because of their intended travels to the caliphate. They ask each other, whether they have ecosystems in place to bail them out from prison in case of capture by law enforcement agencies. Ironically, these conversations and discussions are part of legal documents on court cases against many of these individuals.

More than perhaps ideological indoctrination, it is cult figures such as Baghdadi himself that attract people towards

ISIS. Sirajuddin, in his online pro-ISIS tirades, also seemingly spent considerable time promoting Baghdadi's name for *Time* magazine's Person Of The Year title, oddly, a Western publication, which technically Sirajuddin as a disciple of Islamic State should be dead against. Sirajuddin, according to accounts, asked his online ecosystem to 'hack their [*Time* magazine's] website and declare "Emir ul Momin" (roughly translated to the leader of the believers) Abu Bakr al-Baghdadi as Time's Person of the Year'. He even created memes to further such propaganda on social media.

His account also offers a small yet important window into the family life, and reactions of a family to a member sliding towards radicalization. Families tend to play a very important part in de-radicalization programmes that many Indian states such as Kerala, Andhra Pradesh and so on employ. Sirajuddin talked with his wife via WhatsApp and let her know of his intentions. These chats also revealed that he had a young son. The chats showcased friction between the two, as Sirajuddin clarified to his wife of his aims of being a member of ISIS and travelling to the caliphate. In one of these chats, he revealed to her about his contacts with ISIS, his aim to join the group with or without his family, work towards jannat (heaven) through his deeds done in the name of Islamic State and finally, and perhaps most disturbingly, make his son a mujahid as well.

Sirajuddin's online activities only expanded, and instead of traditional social media such as Facebook, he became more active on Telegram. He was part of a host of Telegram groups, and invited members of the groups that he ran to join other groups as well in order to create a globalized network. He also joined a channel called Caliphate Cyber Army, Elite Section. The members of this group were seemingly mostly techies and hackers, who posted screenshots of successful hackings of websites, mostly those belonging to governments in places such as Libya, Iraq and so on.

A Telegram channel that Sirajuddin became a part of in late 2015 was called HindBattle, with its name being changed to Ghazwathul Hind later on. There were more than 353 members in the said group, including Sirajuddin. However, there is no data available to know whether the members were Indians, South Asians or global, who joined in to support pro-ISIS Indian accounts. Pro-ISIS people joining each other's groups, lists and chat rooms was a common occurrence, a show of support towards the unity of the caliphate and their common aim to travel to this new Islamic proto-state and become a citizen of this land. 'So they are worried about growing power of IS? May Allah cast more terror and fear in their hearts,' Sirajuddin told one Fatimah, an alleged wife of an IS soldier from Buenos Aires. 'Inshallah very soon [travel to caliphate], pray to Allah sister we all die death of a shaheed in Islamic land, keep patience sister and wait for Allah's call. Inshallah sister, we shall do that soon [travel to ISIS territory; Fatimah wanted to travel to Libya]. I am getting a new phone number for Dawlah (another word for Islamic State, with a literal translation being just "the State") work.'

Meanwhile, the Ghazwathul Hind channel became a place to share a multitude of predominantly Indian content, which included pictures of the IC 814 hijack in which a now-defunct Indian Airlines's Airbus A300 operating a flight from Nepal's capital Kathmandu to New Delhi was hijacked and taken to Kandahar in Afghanistan. The event produced historic images of Taliban surrounding the Indian aircraft during the seven-day-long standoff, which ended with the release of Indian passengers and aircraft in exchange for three Pakistan-backed terrorists from Indian prisons. These terrorists since have been blamed for some of the largest terror strikes in India, including the 2001 attack on the parliament in New Delhi and the 2008 attack on Mumbai. Other content shared on this Telegram group included propaganda releases from Al Qaeda in the Indian Subcontinent (AQIS), and pictures from Kashmir of funeral processions of militants killed in the state by security forces, highlighting them as martyrs. Another interesting facet that came up in this group by one of the users was the following statement: 'Only solution for Kashmir is jihad, main factor that will help Kashmir will be the liberation of Afghanistan from invaders (referring to US-led forces). Help Mujahideen in Afghanistan [in] whatever way possible, Kashmir and Palestine are two places, which have been invaded and besieged by kuffar (non-believers). Liberation of Afghanistan is key to free Kashmir, same like Syria to Palestine.' This post, from 2015, oddly resonates with many factors being played out today in theatres such as the USA–Taliban peace negotiations in Doha, which if successful, would lead to Washington surrendering its war against terror back to Taliban, a group it aimed to defeat in its post-9/11 anti-terror programme.

Sirajuddin's online existence and groups also brought him close to some of the top pro-ISIS 'recruiters' online. While the likes of ShamiWitness or Shafi Armar do not figure in the documents relating to the cases against Sirajuddin, one other curious name does feature, that of one Karen Aisha Hamidon, also just known as 'Karen' in the online world. Sirajuddin had joined a WhatsApp group called Ummah Affairs, which was run by Karen, a thirty-six-year-old former air hostess from Taguig City, on the outskirts of Manila, the capital of the Philippines. Karen allegedly specifically targeted people online, mostly men, to join ISIS and travel to the caliphate. Karen was specifically found to be in touch with people from India, and helping them plan their ISIS activities and travels. Being a woman ISIS recruiter had its advantages, as she is accused of laying down honeytraps to lure men into joining ISIS on the pretext of them getting to travel to the caliphate, become fighters and gain access to women. Karen had a wide footprint online in places where Indian and South Asian potentials for ISIS loitered. Whether she was part of a larger structure of online recruitments based on regional strategies by Islamic State or part of an unorganized but well-connected ecosystem of promoting Do-It-Yourself (DIY) jihad remains contested.

Karen also lured people into acting for ISIS by promising marriage to them, and meeting them in the caliphate eventually. Even though she is only directly associated with two Indian cases, she also had chats with Areef Majeeb, with some of their exchanges described as an erotic Mills & Boon novel as she enticed Majeeb to travel to the caliphate, which he eventually did.

However, all was not rosy with Karen's dealings with Indians at least. Sirajuddin had, by the accounts available, a strenuous online relationship with her. Sirajuddin in his talks with various other jihadists online talked about keeping their distance from Karen as she could not be fully trusted, possibly highlighting the fact that he saw her as a spy, an intelligence operator or from a rival jihadist group fighting ISIS. 'I will leave her . . . let this be the final assault,' Sirajuddin said in one of his chats with another online ISIS sympathizer and a group admin called Farasha.

Sirajuddin's distrust of Karen only increased, as in other groups he openly challenged her and the groups she was an admin of. A separate group on Telegram called Karen's Diary existed where users dwelled on who Karen was and what her motivations were. There were screenshots between various group administrators and ISIS sympathizers doing rounds about Karen, one of which allegedly showed Karen outing phone numbers used by Sirajuddin. This pushed Sirajuddin even further to build consensus against Karen amongst the various ISIS groups he was a part of. As a return, one of the other members of the group sent Sirajuddin a screenshot showing Karen's contact details as well. This theatre exposed both Sirajuddin and Karen's contact details, a precarious act that could implicate both in the future by law enforcement agencies, which is precisely what happened.

The trust deficit around Karen was increasing. Sirajuddin, talking to another of his online associates, highlighted the sudden disappearance of another online ISIS entity called Mad Mullah. Rumours around Sirajuddin's circles predicted that he had been arrested, and furthermore, it may have been Karen who had given his identity away. 'Mad Mullah disappeared and there are rumours of [him] being arrested,' he told one person by the online name of Bint Afsheen. 'Maybe she is the one who got him arrested.' He also confided to Afsheen that he did not believe Karen was affiliated to the ISIS in the Philippines, which is one of the few, properly ordained wilayats of Islamic State outside the Middle East. Sirajuddin argued that Karen was in fact working for a rival group, and if she indeed was working for ISIS in the Philippines, the organization should release a clarification of the same on an official group letterhead.

Sirajuddin's concerns over Karen were not superficial. In case she was a spook, and actually had details of his whereabouts, phone numbers and so on, it would mean that he was at a high risk of having his identity revealed. This, perhaps, weighed on his mind more than anything else at that given point of time. Further groups were created on Telegram, being largely invitation based, in some of which Sirajuddin and others decided that groups run by Karen be hacked into and information on her be made public. Karen's India footprint as per reports extended to more than twenty known people, while it will perhaps remain unknown forever of how many Indians exactly, knowingly or unknowingly, she came in contact with.

The Karen vs Sirajuddin saga gives an interesting inside look on both the veracity and importance of Islamic State's online ecosystems. The online ecosystems themselves became an important tool for both information and recruitment for ISIS. As seen above, two administrators, Karen and Sirajuddin had a certain assessment of their own importance within the ISIS digital ecosystems. They pitted each against the other and attempted to push their own agendas forward to try to become the most influential of their peers. The ones directly recruiting, helping move money, or orchestrating safe passage for ISIS recruits have the upper hand, but the ones propagating pro-ISIS agenda on social media are also given near-equal importance. This feeds their ego, and makes them more committed towards the cause even if they're situated in a far away place.

Karen was eventually arrested by authorities in the Philippines, which allowed India's investigative services access to her in order to get more details of her footprint amongst pro-ISIS people in India. According to reports, she mentioned people from places such as Daman and Diu, Kanpur and Kolkata who had come in touch with her wanting to join the Islamic State.[2] India's good relations with the Philippines helped in the investigation of such cases. The Philippines, as mentioned before, is home to an official wilayat of Islamic State, and the military of that country fought a very brutal, and no-holds-barred public battle against this wilayat in Marawi in the Lanao del Sur part of the country. The 'Battle of Marawi', as it is known now, raged for more than five months, officially lasting between May and October of 2017. The Abu Sayyaf group, an Islamist militant organization in the country, like ISIS, gained global spotlight after it officially surrendered its allegiance to ISIS and its caliph. Prior to this, Abu Sayyaf was responsible for the Philippines's worst terror strike in 2004 after it bombed a ferry, which sank, killing more than 100 people. Sayyaf was founded in 1991 and come out of the Moro insurgency in the same part of the country. The Moro groups have been fighting a decades-long war looking to secede their province into an independent nation based on the tenets of Wahabi-Sunni Islam.

In July 2018, the Indian government donated $5,00,000 to the Philippine war against ISIS, most of it earmarked for the rehabilitation efforts of the citizens of Marawi. By this time, the world had recognized that while on the cusp of a geographic defeat, the influence of Islamic State is going to remain, and perhaps even flourish, in the years to come. And closer cooperation on intelligence and military between states was the only way for governments to try and track their citizens who may have fallen for the trappings of this ideological cesspool, which had waged a war on the ground in the Middle East, but was also waging an equally sized information war around the world.

Schrödinger's Thirty-nine

Mosul being overrun by fighters of Islamic State also had an effect in New Delhi, which lies more than 3000 km away from the historic Iraqi city, as news came in of thirty-nine Indian men, mostly labourers working on projects in the region, being taken hostage by ISIS. The newly elected Prime Minister Modi walked into office with this particular crisis brewing in Iraq. Most of the thirty-nine missing were from Punjab, working in these dangerous regions to earn bread for families back home.

Perhaps, at some level, such a crisis was inevitable considering the number of Indians working in the Gulf. Nonetheless, this caused a flurry of activity in New Delhi as the new government scrambled to prove its merit by attempting to save the missing, or at least gain information of their safety. However, little did anyone realize that this issue would become a strange saga of utter confusion, communications breakdown, and bad intelligence lasting more than four years.

As the news broke of the kidnapping of the Indian workers, India dispatched senior diplomat Suresh K. Reddy to Erbil, the capital of the autonomous region of Kurdistan in Iraq, to help newly appointed Indian Ambassador to Baghdad Ajay Kumar with this developing issue. From here, infrastructure was hurriedly put together to tap into defunct diplomatic and intelligence ecosystems that India had employed in Iraq during the Saddam reign, an autocrat who was fairly close to India and had good relations with New Delhi throughout. In fact, even when Saddam's Iraq invaded the tiny emirate of Kuwait announcing the start of the first Gulf War, New Delhi evacuated its embassy staff from Kuwait City not outside the region, but to Basra in southern Iraq knowing that its ties with Saddam would offer a safe passage to its diplomats. 'If there is any one prominent hostage to the convulsive crisis caused by Iraq's invasion of Kuwait, it is Indian diplomacy,' Dilip Bobb wrote in *India Today* in October 1990 as the Basra Hilton became a five-star holding cell for Indian diplomats.[1] India's then Foreign Minister I.K. Gujral became the first non-Arab senior functionary of any government to embrace Saddam. This made for what many analysts regard as one of India's historic foreign policy mistakes in the Middle East, as the picture of the Iraq–India embrace, one that New Delhi thought was aligned with its non-aligned approach to international affairs, was interpreted as Indian ambivalence to Saddam's outright invasion of a neighbouring sovereign state.

So why is this important in the context of Islamic State and the kidnapping of the Indian workers which created drama for years? After the rise of ISIS, and its takeover of territory in Iraq, many former Saddam loyalists and military leaders under the erstwhile President's Ba'athist party joined Islamic State, often in top military or administrative positions. Reddy, who served in Baghdad from 2011 to 2014, was sent back to Iraq in June after finishing his stint in the country just a month earlier to help with the brewing crisis. But why Erbil? And what kind of help could India employ other than diplomatic backing to Baghdad against terrorism?

The Ba'athists had good relations with India, with New Delhi even training Iraqi MiG pilots in the 1970s and 1980s through both Ba'athist leaders' rule in the country, Ahmed Hassan al-Bakr and then Saddam. The training programmes started in 1958, three years before the formal inception of the NAM in Belgrade, former Yugoslavia. Air Marshal Philip Rajkumar in his writings recalled how Indian Air Force cadets arrived in Tikrit, home to the flying academy of the Iraqi Air Force, amidst the Iran–Iraq war in 1981, where Iraqi pilots would train on then Czechoslovakia made Aero Vodochody L-29 and L-39 training jets before moving on to the MiG 21, which India had been flying since 1963.

These levels of cooperation with Saddam under the guise of NAM created goodwill for New Delhi within the Iraqi systems, and the residue of these systems in the post 2003 Iraq conflict is what New Delhi hoped to tap into to gain information on the missing Indians even if they were under capture by Islamic State. This included two particular names, Azhar al-Obeidi and Ahmed al-Rabd Rashid, two former senior functionaries in the Saddam military who were known to have been given charge of setting up Islamic State's institutional systems (religious police, taxation and so on) for the cities Tikrit and Mosul, two of the first big cities to fall to ISIS. This gave a minuscule chance for New Delhi to try and dig up old alliances and diplomatic goodwill that stood between the Ba'athist party and India for decades, in order to try and secure the release of the said workers. Whether anything transpired from attempts to work these old connections remains unknown.

'They were killed, not sure when or where but that is what I am told,' a 'fixer', or local journalist often hired by journalists in the regions around Mosul told this author in late 2014. However, for reasons best known to them, the Modi government decided to remain consistent with the narrative that the thirty-nine people were alive, for the next three years, seemingly waiting for DNA proof before declaring them dead.

In February 2015, External Affairs Minister Sushma Swaraj met family members of the thirty-nine missing for the sixth time, giving them assurances which many analysts tracking the Middle East knew was next to impossible, that the workers were alive and that they would be brought back and that the government was working on it. What perhaps was more baffling than anything else was the repeated stance of the government backing their claims based on multiple sources confirming to them that the workers were alive in ISIS captivity.

'Today is my sixth meeting with them,' Swaraj said. 'Every time when they come, we apprise them with current efforts being made by us to get them released. As I said before, till date we have no evidence if they are alive or dead. But due to the efforts we are putting in, we have been informed by many sources that they are still alive. And we believe that the information is true, so we are still searching for them.'[2]

Fast-forward to May 2015, and Swaraj only doubled down on the claims over the thirty-nine being alive. 'Probably Badush; many died there, many were foreigners,' the journalist helping this author with reporting the rise of ISIS said back then, with conviction, but of course without confirmed sourcing. But increasingly, factoring in the nature of the conflict, it was becoming glaringly obvious that even for ISIS, keeping a group of thirty-nine people together is highly risky, considering the level of aerial surveillance against them was quite intense. Not to mention, keeping thirty-nine people together, alive, supplying food, water, without making any specific demands for their release and so on, was pointing towards the fact that the workers had not survived, or at the very least, were not together. It did not require deep-intelligence based information to understand basic designs of warfare, that keeping big groups of detainees even in a proto-state or captured territory is a hazard for a terror or insurgent group.

Nonetheless, India persisted with its line of not knowing whether these citizens were dead or alive, but some sort of intelligence suggesting that they are alive. 'So far as the thirty-nine Indians are concerned, it is my constant endeavour. I have eight sources, not just one or two, who say they are still alive. These sources are not just something said by somebody. I have written information and have shared it with the Prime Minister, with the minister from Punjab Harsimrat Kaur Badal also,' Swaraj committed further. The MEA's confidence on its sources and the government's relentlessness to pursue this line of argument remains baffling to this day. Officials themselves offer little clarity, and seem to have genuinely believed that some sort of intelligence was perhaps provided by a friendly country in the region.

However, a completely different turn of events was taking place parallel to Swaraj's statements in the form of one Harjit Masih, a resident of Punjab's Kala Afghana village, a few kilometres north of Amritsar, who was one of the survivors of the group of forty labourers who were abducted from University Lake Towers in Mosul. But Masih's account of what happened to the thirty-nine was suppressed, and according to reports, he was kept under the supervision of intelligence agencies and shifted between Gurgaon, Noida and Bengaluru.

Masih's account, first reported expertly by journalist Alia Allana, was simple; he confirmed that ISIS executed the thirty-nine workers in front of him on 15 June 2014, four days after they had been rounded up.[3] Masih recalled that all of them had been taken to a railway crossing, around a ravine, asked to kneel, and shot dead. However, the bullet shot towards Masih had only grazed him, after which he fell to the ground and played dead until the area was clear. He then hitchhiked his way out with a good samaritan who dropped him somewhere near Erbil. Masih was then picked up by an Indian official situated at the post in Erbil specifically made for this task (the Erbil consulate was officially inaugurated only in August 2016, with the repatriation of the thirty-nine as its main mandate at that time, after Reddy's departure as special envoy in early 2015, who was replaced by two young officials, Sanjay Rana, a Joint Secretary officer with experience in the region along with Abu Mathen George, a young diplomat fluent in Arabic).[4]

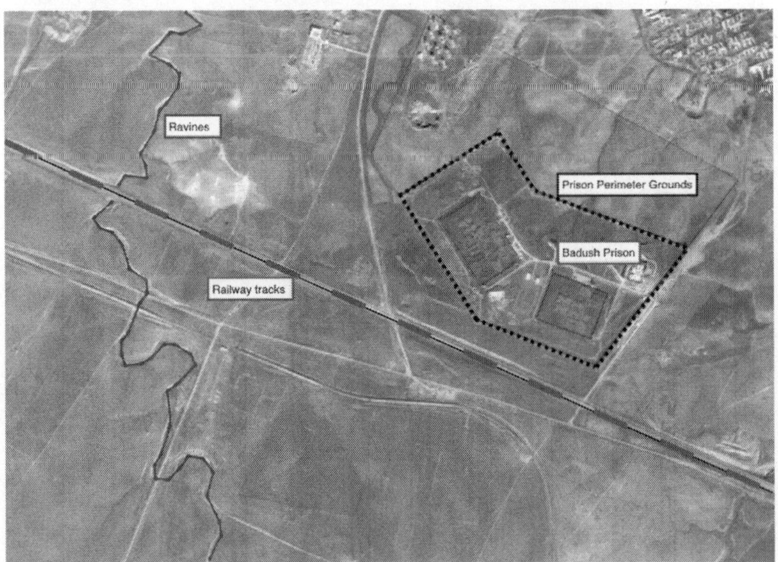

(Figure 3: A map showing the immediate surrounding area around Badush prison where the thirty-nine Indians were executed by ISIS)

Masih was told not to confirm or talk about the killings, while at the same time the Indian government went ahead with its version of 'Schrödinger's thirty-nine', keeping the missing people dead and alive at the same time while dragging the families along, keeping their hopes up against all odds. India's Minister of State for External Affairs, General V.K. Singh, a former chief of the Indian Army, visited Iraq on more than one occasion to push forward New Delhi's search.

Masih had left home to become part of the more than seven million people who leave Indian shores for the Middle East to find work. Masih's initial plan was Dubai, as is for most people travelling westward, however he ended up in Iraq where wages were higher, but dangers were even more so. The route for Masih was similar to the one taken by hundreds of young Indian men every year, via a mixture of agents looking to make a quick buck in what could best be described as modern-day, subtle labour trade. Masih ended up in Basra instead of Dubai, and later in Mosul as the promise to work in the southern Iraqi city ended up not being true.

In Mosul, the forty of them, looking to find work, were unaware that they were entering what was to become one of ISIS's main cities, where governance of Baghdad was to be replaced by hard-line Sunni militants who were not particularly fond of foreigners, specifically non-Muslims. The boys from Punjab were in trouble from the moment they entered Mosul.

The group soon found itself kidnapped by ISIS (or affiliated militants) and even though initially they were able to contact family members back home, the communication soon fell silent. According to the accounts narrated by Masih in the media, while everyone was still telling each other that they were being treated well, panic struck when the militants asked the Indians (not the

Bangladeshis who were also being held in the compound) to accompany them. From Mosul, the Indians were put in a trailer and driven for about an hour before reaching the barren land around railway lines where other militants were waiting. The captured Indians were asked to kneel, ignoring their pleas for mercy and offers to even convert to Islam in return for freedom, and then they were shot dead. As luck would have it, Masih was able to fake his way out. The location of these killings in all probability was just outside Badush prison, where railway lines run mere metres away from the boundary walls. Five days earlier, in the same prison compound, ISIS had reportedly killed more than 600 Shia prisoners being held there after segregating the Sunnis from Shias. In March 2017, after Mosul's liberation and Iraqi forces' regaining control of the city, it was confirmed that mass graves were discovered around the compound. These findings confirmed a Human Rights Watch report from October 2014 that highlighted that ISIS herded up more than 1,500 people on to trucks and drove them to the regions around Badush about 2 km away from the prison where these killings took place. During these massacres, like Masih, there were other survivors as well. According to other survivor accounts, the ISIS militants only stopped after they had run out of bullets, making sure that those executed were actually dead. One of the witnesses described that thirty to forty people had managed to survive.[5]

On 20 March 2018, it was finally confirmed by the Indian government that the thirty-nine Indians were indeed killed in Badush by ISIS. Swaraj told the Indian parliament: 'With full proof I can say these thirty-nine are dead. We wanted to give the families closure only after concrete proof.' General Singh along with an Indian Air Force's C-17 Globemaster heavy-lift aircraft departed Delhi for Mosul to bring back the mortal remains of the thirty-nine Indians, who had died in 2014, and their remains found around the Badush prison compound. DNA testing confirmed that the graves found of the thirty-nine were indeed those of the missing Indian men, putting an end to a distressing saga lasting four years for the families of the victims.

As the government explained the fate of the thirty-nine, Masih's account largely stood vindicated. From the phone calls made to the families by the victims to how they were killed, there never really was a reason (beyond basic intelligence checks) to doubt his account. The government never did divulge as to what those 'many' sources were (some, we know, were humanitarian agencies working on the ground) that it repeatedly referenced to over the three years as proof that the workers were in fact alive. More than anything else, this infliction of hope on to the families who in many cases relied on these men for their livelihoods was avoidable. If local journalists in the Mosul region heard of the Badush massacre and had news about Indians also being killed back in 2014 itself, there is no reason why the government of India needed nearly half a decade to confirm the same, even if ISIS had become the prevalent force in Mosul.

'They used a piece of wood to light the fire. They used it as a torch to burn the dead bodies and to see who was dead and who was alive. When they approached me, one of the Da'ish [ISIS] terrorists told someone that I was still breathing, so after I got shot in my arm, they shot two more bullets into my legs . . . When it was my turn, they set my right leg on fire. But I had to withstand the pain so they wouldn't know that I was still breathing. When they saw I didn't move, they told each other that I was dead. Then they burned the person next to me,' another survivor of the Badush killings, only documented as 'M.A' to protect his identity, recounted.[6]

This case was perhaps India's biggest tryst with Islamic State. It involved one of the main tenets and fears of the Indian diplomacy as far as the country's foreign policy in the Middle East goes, that of protecting its diaspora. Micromanaging a giant workforce abroad is not easy; nonetheless, the government's approach to portray itself as a saviour of Indians who live abroad, with Swaraj playing the role of a counsellor via Twitter, addressing individual grievances in some strange role play of a godmother, ultimately came to little use when actual diplomatic and strategic depth had been challenged in what was an immensely dangerous and dire situation in Mosul. The Indian diplomatic access in the Middle East is a globally enviable asset, and very few countries around the world have the same pull. Despite the same, nothing short of a circus was created by the government around the thirty-nine, while the sole survivor, a poor labourer, was asked to remain silent according to his own reported account.

The first actual case of ISIS's effect on India was not Kashmir, or another part of the country susceptible to such ideologies and religious brainwashing, but Punjab, a story of migration to foreign lands to escape economic destitution. This threw light on the fact that the seven million plus Indians in the larger Middle East region, who send back billions of dollars for the Indian economy and their homes more often than not do so at great peril and price, and highlighted the failures of our own economics and policies.

From Kashmir to Kerala: ISIS and its Narratives

It is perhaps normal for a generalized analysis on where an organization such as ISIS could have the most influence in India to underline Kashmir as the most volatile option. This preconditioned thinking is still highlighted in debates on ISIS's effects on India, as minuscule as they may be. The Indian discourse knows terrorism via the lens of Kashmir, and global Islamist groups have almost never featured as valid threats from this context. For India, many of the problems relating to terrorism are ingrained in local political and societal grievances.

Despite generalizations suggesting that it would in fact be Kashmir that would be most susceptible to ISIS's global outreach, this hypothesis has come out as not true. It is in fact, the southern Indian state of Kerala that has clocked up the most number of pro-ISIS cases in the country. Why does one of India's most prosperous states, with the highest levels of literacy anywhere in the country, have the most number of such cases? The answers are in fact rooted in migration, economics, and religion. But more on Kerala later.

'Gar firdaus bar-rue zamin ast, hami asto, hamin asto, hamin ast.' It is said that this was the line narrated by the great Mughal emperor Jahangir about Kashmir. Translated, it reads: 'If there is a heaven on earth, it is here, it is here, it is here.' The Kashmir Valley, nestled deep in the Himalayas, gives any other mountainous region in the world a run for its money. However, the Valley has also been home to decades-long strife, one that seems to have no end in sight. Home to the nucleus behind the tensions between India and Pakistan, with Islamabad resorting to using terrorism as a state-sponsored policy against New Delhi in attempts to capture the narrative amongst the majority Muslim population in the state, it is the Valley that many feared was the most susceptible to falling prey to the 'globalist' agenda of the Islamic State.

In the summer of 2014, a map started to do rounds on the vast pro-ISIS online networks on social media. It allegedly outlined the group's vision of what Islamic State should look territorially by 2020. Captured by the mainstream media, this map made it on most news channels across the world as it showed vast swathes of Africa, southern Europe, Central Asia and South Asia as part of what ISIS was hoping would be land eventually ruled by it. India, Pakistan, and Afghanistan were clubbed under the 'Khurasan' tag. The map was one of the first instances of propaganda that overtly 'targeted' India and highlighted that the South Asian region is at the back of the mind for ISIS as well.

(Figure 4: The map circulated by ISIS supporters in 2014–15)

The Kashmir crisis is also a creator of political and societal vacuum, the exact kind of situation that a group such as ISIS thrives in, and the one it found in Syria and pockets of Iraq during the 2014–15 period. There was no denying that Indian intelligence and law enforcement agencies alike were alarmed at the rise of ISIS, and the non-traditional means it was employing to not just radicalize the youth ideologically, but pushing them to commit acts of terror, and also to radicalize their friends and create ecosystems for ISIS to tap into at a later stage if need be. A lot of this alarm was based around Kashmir, and perhaps for valid reasons. Srinagar is a city which can be equated to a traditional South Asian pressure cooker, a steel chamber closed off from all sides with a lid on top which allows pressure to escape only when needed, with heat simmering inside at a high intensity. The situation in the state has been precarious over the past two to three years, after a prolonged lull in militant violence lasting months.

In February 2019, this author landed in Srinagar to research how the ideas behind terrorism were evolving in the Valley between localized militancy of Pakistan-based groups such as Lashkar-e-Taiba and Jaish-e-Mohammed and transnational jihadist groups such as Al Qaeda and ISIS. It is important to note here that committing an act of terror by an individual emerges from a kaleidoscope of political, social, ideological, and geographical micro-factors. A region under the effects of terrorism has signatures of the above-mentioned metrics unique to that particular conflict, geography, or demography.

Srinagar during the month of February was under the spell of clear air and fresh snow, and looked set to give any other mountain resort town on the planet very stiff competition. The drive from the airport to the central parts of the town gives one a quick glimpse of the prevailing situation on the ground. Soldiers of the Indian armed and paramilitary forces along with the police could be spotted every few hundred metres. The citizens of Kashmir went along with their daily chores, crisscrossing around these soldiers who kept a strong eye on the people and their movements. The level of visibility of the armed forces had been increased after two major terror strikes in India in 2016, starting with a terror attack on the Pathankot air base in the state of Punjab which looked to target the Indian Air Force's aircraft on the ground. The terrorists, who were wearing army fatigues at the time of the strike, were blamed by India to be members of JeM, despite the same being claimed by a group calling itself the United Jihad Council. Later in the same year, after global outcry against JeM and Pakistan on the attacks, militants targeted another military installation, this time in Uri,

Jammu and Kashmir, in which nineteen Indian troops were killed. At the time, this was designated as the worst terror attack on the Indian armed forces in two decades. Here, once again, JeM's name as the group behind the violence was raised. In brief, these are the dynamics of violence in the state of Kashmir, and until now global jihadist groups such as Al Qaeda have had next to no success, and not for the lack of trying.

At the helm of Srinagar's gorgeous scenery and dark history is the Dal Lake, a body of water synonymous with the very identity of Kashmir. It is a famous tourist spot, with locally made boats, known as shikaras, and houseboats that are popular with tourists lined up waiting to showcase the best of what nature has to offer there. The promenade around the lake has next to no standing space for cars or people, signalling that the security apparatus does not want big crowds, specifically of cars, to line up anywhere in the town. The surrounding area is peppered with tea stalls, snack stalls and shops selling local produce and Kashmiri crafts' items. As we walked around, and stopped at a tea shop for a drink, a few steps over, on a shuttered down shop, the words 'ISIS will win' were graffitied. The graffiti, when examined closely, looked fresh; it was perhaps a day old. An Indian Army convoy truck rolled in right next to the shop, to pick up boats belonging to the military which were placed in the Dal Lake a day earlier to facilitate Prime Minister Narendra Modi's visit to the state. According to the locals, Kashmiris were moved away from the lake during Modi's visit, shops were closed, mobile internet was shut down, and boatsmen were asked to not come to work. Despite the ISIS graffiti bang in the centre of the town, in its biggest tourist spot, the Army did not bother much about it. 'Must be some local kids; they probably don't mean it. Sometimes they also do this to mess with the police,' a local sitting in front of the tea stall said. The 'probably' part of his sentence is perhaps what gives the security officials night terrors in a state with as precarious a security situation as Kashmir.

Driving around Srinagar, there is a forever-lingering sense of tension. In the town's old quarters, where even as you drive by, fellow pedestrians and motorists who are sharing the road with you can recognize you as being an outsider within minutes. This is the part of the town which is steeped in history, and many locals here are of the view that they're largely fed up with both India and Pakistan, which seems to be the driving narrative of *azaadi*, or freedom, looking for a sovereign state of Kashmir.

The old town, on this day, seems relatively empty, once again an effect of the Prime Minister's visit to Srinagar, which means that the policing on the streets is much stricter than any other average day. The Valley has seen its share of armed forces vs the people moments in the recent past, some of which have overflowed into national outrage. These include both locals pelting stones at security convoys and the armed forces taking extreme actions against the locals, such as the incident where Indian Army's Major Leetul Gogoi caused a national outcry after he tied a local Kashmiri in front of his jeep as a human shield in 2017. Some believe events such as these have at times forced local youths to look towards Islamic State as a potential safe haven.

In this old part of Srinagar stands the epic Jamia Masjid, which was commissioned by Sultan Sikander in 1394 CE, and stands imposing in the part of Srinagar which is known to be the heart of the town's political-theological thinking. The Masjid is a site to behold, and is an architectural masterpiece. As we headed towards the mosque, the snow had made it difficult for most to bother with opening their shops. Black ice had formed on the roads and the pathway towards the mosque. The gates led to a small cluster of shops, which were open, waiting for the few tourists who may brave the inclement weather. However, what caught our eye there was, once again, the graffiti. 'ISIS town', a thin graffiti in black spray paint somewhat camouflaged amidst the colour of the wall. 'This is normal,' said a prominent Delhi-based researcher to me when I raised this query with him. Most studying the Valley, and even many we encountered who live in the Valley, do not see these graffiti slogans on walls in prominent places in Srinagar as a threat, but as a fad, one that will stop once it runs out its course. But this was not limited to Srinagar, on the outskirts of Srinagar, amidst graffiti that say 'Indian dogs go home' and 'Indian Army go home', a few concrete pillars supporting unfinished highways and bridges, where no one seemed to be working, also said 'ISIS home land'.

Despite these observations, it remains true that ISIS has next to no capital in the Valley. It is important to recognize that ISIS is a powerful brand, and spraying such statements in an extremely volatile region such as Kashmir will ruffle feathers not only in the Indian security establishment, but the secessionist and anti-India Islamist groups backed by Pakistan as well.

A few months after the declaration of the Islamic State by Baghdadi, in late 2014, flags that looked similar to those of ISIS's 'black flag' started to make appearances on the streets of Srinagar. This, expectedly, made front-page news across the country.[1] Some of the flags from the Kashmir streets shown in the videos had the letters 'ISJK' inscribed on them, seemingly making a reference to an entity called Islamic State Jammu and Kashmir (ISJK). However, in other instances, the flags being waved seemed to have only taken inspiration from the ISIS flag but

('ISIS Town' sprayed on the boundary walls of Jamia Masjid, Srinagar, February 2019. Photograph by author)

were poor homemade copies that did not even have the correct symbols and imagery from the flag. In one instance, one of the flags being waved as that of ISIS more closely resembled those of groups that were linked with the Tehrik-i-Taliban Pakistan (TTP) and other Taliban aligned groups, and not ISIS. In fact, both the TTP and Afghan Taliban are at odds with ISIS and have been fighting their influence, specifically in Afghanistan. One of the flags initially waved was the classic 'black flag' with just 'Allah' and 'Taliban' written on it, while another, in one of the instances, borrowed imagery from Al Qaeda instead of ISIS, again a set of jihadist groups at odds with each other.[2]

The Indian media's loose understanding of information as a tool of coercion, and the questionable ethical editorial practices of the numerous TV channels that crowd the airwaves today act as an amplifier for uncorroborated information being peddled under the guise of 'news'. While the 'ISJK' tagged flags appeared in just a handful of cases, the ISJK moniker started getting space in the public discourse as media reports started to use it to refer to cases of ISIS flags in the Valley. To put it in perspective, perhaps one or two miscreants, who wrote 'ISJK' on flags and were photographed during stone-pelting incidents or protests against security personnel, managed to create a national narrative, and perhaps more dangerously, a sub-brand for ISIS itself to exploit. Since October 2014 when these flag incidents took place, ISJK managed to become a small, yet standalone brand in the Valley with the actual Islamic State having nothing to do with it.

The Kashmir law enforcement establishment didn't help the case. Instead of unquestionably dispelling the ISJK as a non-existent entity, they managed to bolster it by telling reporters that some of the terror attacks may have been by ISJK. The then police chief of Jammu and Kashmir, S.P. Vaid, made the erroneous strategic mistake of admitting the existence of an ISJK to the press in June 2018.[3] Just three months earlier, in March 2018, Vaid had said that there is no ISIS in the state,[4] a statement which the Ministry of Home Affairs had also made a month earlier.[5]

In February 2018, a militant by the name of Eisa Fazili shot and killed Farooq Ahmad, a constable of Jammu and Kashmir Police tasked with the duty of being a part of the security of moderate-separatist leader Fazal Haq Qureshi in the Soura suburb of Srinagar. This was the second such shooting in the area allegedly done by ISIS, with the first one turning into a shoot-out in November 2017, which led to the death of an assistant sub-inspector of the police and a local militant. The case of Eisa Fazili, however, offers the perfect example of how ISIS played global institutions on its narrative wars, and was able to cause disruptions in law enforcement and counterterrorism strategies merely with a few social media accounts.

Fazili was what one could term as a 'freelance jihadist', who had fallouts with local radical groups leaving him out of these ecosystems and to fend for himself. He was reportedly a student of engineering at the Baba Ghulam Shah Badshah University in Rajouri, around 180 km south of Srinagar, amidst a marked increase in radicalization in the southern parts of the state where a new battle between politics and religion has started to take shape. Fazili's radicalization had happened much before he killed the policeman.

After shooting the policeman, Fazili got in touch with ISIS's Amaq News Agency and stated that he had committed an attack in the name of ISIS. A few hours later, Amaq released a statement via its Telegram channel claiming the attack.

As we dissect this case, most information available points towards the fact that Fazili was not known to ISIS prior to this case, and ISIS was not aware of his attack plans either. It just took one act of violence and one e-mail for him, and one acknowledgment from Amaq to 'become ISIS'.

Fazili, like many others we have highlighted before, used social media to let his newly mushrooming thoughts be known to the world and his immediate circle. Coming from a modest family in Kashmir, it is most likely that his parents or other family elders were either not on social media or were blocked by him from seeing his posts, which gave him the confidence to speak his mind.

His friend and classmate, Aamir Ahmad Amin, wrote a post on Facebook mourning the passing of his friend, highlighting details of how he was slipping towards the jihadist narrative and getting radicalized, having fights in school over religious discussions and a fast developing intolerance against criticism of ISIS by his friends and family. Some important and poignant sections of Amin's writing on Fazili are as follows:

'Eisa's comments on my Facebook posts over the years are still visible I think, and a keen observer will be able to gauge out a transition towards hard-core radicalism in his beliefs. Back in school, him and his like-minded friends would often have arguments with other classmates and teachers about religion, and I remember the fiery expression on Eisa's face when someone criticized the then newly mushroomed cult we all know today as ISIS. During the same period, our Missionary school authorities had refused to leave a time gap or allow students to go for Zuhr prayers, which further fueled their anger and protest until a stalemate was eventually reached. This should give everyone a faint idea of how Eisa perceived this "zulm" on Muslims, superimposed on the backdrop of HRVs [Human Rights Violations] in Kashmir and a belief strengthened by his interpretation of the countless other events across the world.

'I curse the Wahabi preachers who mislead [sic] him, the Tehreeki leaders who inspired and encouraged him, the careless relatives and friends who never stopped him from taking the leap into the dark abyss. They are all alive and well today—ranting and raving—but Eisa is not. They will all have breakfast with their families tomorrow, continue with their daily chores and very soon return back to their normal lives of happiness and laughter—but he will not.

. . . The fact is, had Eisa been born in some far away land, in another happy and peaceful region of the world, he would have certainly pursued a different road and lived to tell a different tale. His sad demise, more importantly, draws attention to the bitter truth that the shrill cries of people today will once again fall to deaf ears in the larger politico-religious game of death and destruction that the Kashmir Issue truly is,' a distraught Amin wrote.[6]

Fazili was killed in an encounter with security forces a month later. At his funeral, where his body was wrapped in an ISIS flag, hundreds attended, underscoring the socio-political undercurrents causing tectonic shifts in the Valley today. It is these political vacuums, just like those in Iraq and Syria, where groups such as ISIS manage to build space and narratives for them.

To understand these situations better, we will have a look at the case of one of the ISIS flag-bearers in Kashmir—who he was, why he did it and what he aimed to achieve and perhaps most importantly, why he travelled all the way from West Bengal to raise an ISIS flag in Kashmir.

‘I am in the News with an ISIS Flag’

Mohammed Mosiuddin, alias Abu Musa, was born in 1990 and ran a grocery shop in West Bengal’s Burdwan area.[1] Mosiuddin was allegedly also in contact with two other locals who were reported to be his conspirators, and shared a common interest in radicalized ideas specially those being perpetrated by the so-called Islamic State. According to accounts, their initial goals were localized, to conduct attacks within West Bengal targeting predominantly Hindu localities. He had started to collect knives, machetes and other such comparatively easily procurable weapons to conduct attacks in the future.

Mosiuddin’s behavioural traits, approach, and radical ideological thinking made him a perfect candidate for an Islamist group to take advantage of. However, his story, or the story of ‘Abu Musa Al Bangali’ as he became known amidst ISIS circles online, was only escalating as he became a pro-ISIS potential being handled by two jihadist organizations, ISIS on one side, and the Jamaat-ul-Mujahideen Bangladesh (JMB) on the other.

JMB is an Islamist organization from Bangladesh, formed in 1998 by Sheikh Abdur Rahman, a radical and former leader of the banned terror group Jagrata Muslim Janata Bangladesh (JMJB). Since its formation, JMB has been at the centre of Islamist attacks and cases of radicalizing Bangladeshi youth, and it started to establish more intricate linkages with ISIS around the 2014–15 period. In 2005, JMB conducted a synchronized strike in Bangladesh, of the likes the country had not witnessed before. JMB detonated around 460 bombs in a span of thirty minutes at 300 different locations, in sixty-three out of Bangladesh's 64 total districts. The outcome of these strikes was Dhaka conducting nearly 700 arrests around the country, including Rahman. In 2007, along with other members of the JMB, Rahman was executed.[2]

In 2015, ISIS's propaganda publication *Dabiq* published an article titled 'The revival of Jihad in Bengal'. In it, 'ISIS Bangladesh' is reported to have killed two foreign nationals in Bangladesh, one from Italy and one from Japan, calling them 'crusaders'. The article also attacked the 'secular' nature of the Awami League government claiming that it 'twisted facts and played the blame game'. This highlights the fact that the narration of this article comes from a Bangladeshi, perhaps in ISIS ranks in Syria or operating remotely but having clout within the hierarchy.

The curious point in the article was the fact that 'Bangladesh' was constantly mentioned only as 'Bengal', which if done so by design, gives precedence to the fact that the target was not just Bangladesh, but Bengali society, culture and plurality which would include the state of West Bengal in India.

One Abu Sulaiman, a suspected Bangladeshi JMB–ISIS crossover radical allegedly played a significant role in pursuing

Mosiuddin to prepare and conduct acts of terror in the name of Islamic State. Attempts to radicalize Mosiuddin further escalated when, once again, Shafi Armar came into the picture and got in touch with both Mosiuddin and Sulaiman in Bangladesh. This suddenly became an international attempt to make Mosiuddin a 'lone wolf'-like attacker, perhaps on the Indian side, to complement the aims of JMB/JMJB.

Mosiuddin was already in touch with pro-ISIS radicals via Facebook and Skype in 2014. Armar came in touch with Mosiuddin around the same period, and started to send propaganda material to Mosiuddin, which included content from academic repositories such as Jihadology.net (Jihadology is a website of curated jihadist literature and materials maintained by researcher and academic Aaron Zelin, for the benefit of the academic community studying jihadism, counterterrorism etc. It is currently banned in India after it was named in testimonies by pro-ISIS individuals as the place where they accessed jihadist material from), Al Shabaab Media, and like many other such cases, lectures from former Al Qaeda ideologue Anwar al-Awlaki.

The discussions that Mosiuddin had on social media and online voice platforms with the likes of Armar revolved around the injustices that Muslims faced across the world, which emboldened his resolve to work for the caliphate and undertake travel to join ISIS in Syria. However, for a small time grocery shop owner from West Bengal, this was not an easy task to achieve. Nonetheless, to keep his morale high, Armar and Sulaiman pushed him to increase his levels of radicalization using the barb of setting up a caliphate there itself, and installing sharia law in the region.

Mosiuddin also gloated that he had the allegiance of two other people, who were close to him. During this period, Armar started to give Mosiuddin tasks, one of which included a reconnaissance trip to the capital New Delhi and then onwards to Srinagar, Kashmir, to survey possible attack locations specifically targeting foreign tourists. He stayed at a hotel near Dal Lake using a false name for two days, and the rest of the time with an unknown local. In New Delhi, he stayed around the Shakarpur area, whether in a hotel or with someone remains uncertain.

Mosiuddin was in Kashmir for one month, during a period when unrest on the streets was palpable as clashes between stone-pelters and security forces were intensifying. During this periodical chaos on the streets of Srinagar, Mosiuddin donned a face mask and entered the streets with intentions to wave the flag of ISIS, which he successfully did. However, the reaction by the locals and protesters who were around him was not necessarily pleasant. In the battle of narratives, one more player playing an ace of spades had absorbed all the attention. And this is precisely what happened. Mosiuddin went to the pro-ISIS groups on Telegram that he was part of and displayed news clippings available on public platforms of him waving ISIS flags during the protest.

But perhaps Mosiuddin's experience was not as good as he might have hoped for. The ISIS flag may have attracted detractors and locals who did not want these images to be shown in the media as it would dilute the larger Kashmiri protest narrative. According to some accounts, Mosiuddin, like a few others who had waved ISIS or ISJK flags, faced hostility on the streets. In his chats, he called the Kashmiri mujahids as 'impure' as they were not aligned with the idea of fighting for Islam and for Muslims, but were more interested in fighting for the land. This, like Sirajuddin earlier, disappointed Mosiuddin leading him to go back to his original ideas of conducting local attacks against Hindus and eventually travel to join the Islamic State.

After the disappointment of Kashmir, Mosiuddin set his sights once again on travelling to Syria to fight in the holy war. He also talked about alternatively travelling to Libya, which would have been comparatively easier to enter. However, his biggest obstacle for this move to take place, ironically (or comically) came in the shape of the Indian bureaucracy in getting a passport. His attempts to pass Indian paperwork in order to get a passport were futile due to abnormalities in permanent address records and so on. He repeatedly asked Armar to provide help in getting the documentation done, and at a point bribing officials to get the paperwork through was also considered. Alternatives explored beyond this were getting a fake passport, as Mosiuddin said he was not getting the passport as he was a Muslim.

Beyond this, talk of acquiring weapons also came up as he was asked to see if AK-47 rifles, ISIS's preferred gun, was available for purchase.

Mosiuddin kept himself up-to-date with how India was dealing with ISIS as well. Online, he chatted about how many pro-ISIS arrests India had made in recent times, highlighting that the country was fearing ISIS and also made up numbers, perhaps to gloat about his knowledge and generally try to impress the other members of the chat group. He told the group that ISIS had 10,000 members in India, which was false and there was no basis for the number to be considered factual. Nonetheless, his conviction towards radicalized thinking made him a candidate that people such as Armar and Sulaiman would tap into to push for localized attacks in the name of ISIS in India, or for that matter, any region in the world possible.

Sulaiman, meanwhile, remains a rather hidden figure in the documentations available. Uncorroborated reports suggest that Armar and him talked about a plan where Sulaiman could go to West Bengal through the legal route of taking a commercial flight from Dhaka to Kolkata and meet Mosiuddin and others in the region, transfer funds and help them in conducting local terror attacks. Mosiuddin by this time had already requested for information on how to make explosive belts and other such paraphernalia.

The other facet that Mosiuddin brought up in his chats in ISIS groups was his hatred for Hindus. He actively talked about Indian Hindu socio-political groups such as the Vishva Hindu Parishad (VHP) and Rashtriya Swayamsevak Sangh (RSS), and equated their rise in Indian politics to a 'doomsday' for Muslims. His targets, from the beginning, were to be either Hindus or foreigners. One of his plans involved using pepper spray to blind a target before killing the person with a knife. Interestingly, this is also a type of attack seen both in the West and in Bangladesh, the former done in the name of ISIS and latter seen in Bangladesh and other parts as well. These tactics have more to do with the availability of locally made, legal weapons that do not involve purchasing firearms, which could alert the authorities. He also planned an attack on Mother Teresa House in Kolkata, due to the number of foreigners that visit the place.

Despite being radicalized to the hilt by coming into contact with both Armar and Sulaiman, Mosiuddin failed to operationalize any of his ideas. Armar, for whom Mosiuddin was just another possibility for increasing ISIS's reach in the subcontinent, had another failed attempt on his hands. However, both the cases highlighted in this book, that of Sirajuddin and Mosiuddin, show that the threat of ISIS to Kashmir was unstructured, disjointed and based more on paranoia than factual development of an ideological ecosystem in the state.

The fact that officers such as S.P. Vaid see-sawed on using the term 'ISJK' in statements and interactions with the press muddled the case even further, and created an unnecessary wedge in the door for use of the term ISJK by the media and others. The reasoning behind Vaid's statements on 'ISJK' is contested. However, two theories could be propped up on why this line was taken by the top cop. First is, of course, that intelligence existed and some sort of hierarchical structure related to ISIS was found to being developed. Second, which analysts believe to have been more plausible, was that by labelling militants under the banner of 'ISIS', it would be easy for security officials to finish them in encounters and anti-terror operations without any major questions being raised.

Either way, these apparent strategies were problematic from the get-go and, if anything, highlighted the big gaps within the security architectures of both Jammu and Kashmir as a state and the Indian government at the centre in understanding what ISIS is and how it operates and what it has done to the war of narratives and information. These gaps in understanding global terror threats pose a significant security risk in a place such as Jammu and Kashmir, where the boundaries of radicalization between religion and politics have started to blur, a departure from the usual type of militancy based around the India–Pakistan conundrum, a point even highlighted by the pro-ISIS individuals studied in this book.

From not just a Kashmiri context, but a pan-Indian one, the differentiation of committing a terror attack in the name of ISIS and one that is committed by ISIS is extremely important to understand. Eisa Fazili's case showed how a 'freelance jihadist' went from nothing to something through one e-mail. The battle of perceptions and stories in the Valley are often played out too close to real life, even if they may be fiction either created by militants or the state.

Narrating Kashmir and Terror

The narrative war in itself changed dramatically in Kashmir with the advent of social media, cheap Chinese-made smartphones and possibly the world's lowest charges for mobile data to access the internet. This advent of modern technology, which is known for bringing economic benefits, societal change for the better and access to a world beyond one's own world, is today criticized for taking away jobs, reducing people-to-people contact, the rigors of traditional media and so on. Kashmir was no different; as it gained increasing access to high-speed internet, the youth of the state—facing unemployment and seclusion amidst the kerfuffle of India–Pakistan, militancy, cross-border terrorism and the failure of separatist narratives and politicians—found through the smartphone an uninterrupted window to the outside world.

This new access is of course double-edged, as useful for the general population as it is for militants to reach out to the general population with much ease. The accessibility of the militancy to the youth in the region is relatively new, and can be traced to Burhan Wani, a young Hizbul Mujahideen commander who offered a completely different approach to connect with the youth of the Valley in order to be more accessible to them and motivate them towards the path of radicalization and an anti-India ideology. Wani's rise was perhaps accidental, as reports suggested that the young militant, at the time in his teens, was killed in an encounter in 2013. The news of his killing at the hands of the Indian military elevated his status, as is often the case (former Al Qaeda leader Anwar al-Awlaki's sermons became much more popular after his killing in 2011 in Yemen) and Wani became a household name. 'Burhan's aim was freedom from India, and I endorse that aim as well,' Wani's father, Muzaffar Wani, said during an interview nine months before the Hizbul militant was killed by security forces in south Kashmir in July 2016.[1]

Wani's modus operandi was what we now see as 'marketable-jihad'. The internet is a mostly unregulated platform. There are hundreds of millions of people connected and the web does not discriminate on economic class or any other such basis anymore. It is affordable for the majority of the citizenry of this planet, which gives a massive canvas to paint for anyone who is capable of holding on to a certain number of people's imagination, whether that be a politician, an artist, a musician, or a terrorist. It was no different in Kashmir.[2]

Wani was perhaps the first militant in Kashmir to use social media and the internet to bolster his name and image openly. After being catapulted to some fame after the false news of his death, Wani capitalized on it and moving away from traditional militant media outputs, made himself and his Hizbul members much more accessible to the public of Kashmir. Wani moved away from the norm, and openly showcased his face choosing not to hide his identity. He produced videos of him and other

Hizbul members roaming around in Kashmir openly, showing their daily lives, them having fun, laughing and cheering. Some videos show them gathered around a fire during winter seasons, taking selfies and videos of each other with smiles on their faces. Wani is shown wearing earphones, most likely listening to music. It also shows Hizbul members wearing clothes similar to those of military fatigues. On the streets of Srinagar, painted across on walls and pillars between graffiti that says 'ISIS town' are words 'Wani is a hero, 'Wani victory', 'Indian dogs go home' and so on. This becomes more visible as you leave the clasps of Srinagar and venture towards south Kashmir. 'The situation of south Kashmir is out of hand; in any other country this territory may be seen as lost,' a local official of the administration said under his breath.

The fact that these videos and images had a distribution platform, with a ready audience, brought about this change of approach to accessibility, and Wani spearheaded it. While there is no empirical proof, or possibility, to ascertain whether Wani and his cohorts were influenced by the way information was being weaponized by the likes of ISIS, Hayat Tahrir al-Sham (HTS) and others in the Middle East, it would be safe to presume that these new avenues of radicalization were being used because they often bypass (or at least did for many years) governmental and intelligence oversight. Wani's popularity as a young and 'cool' militant found many takers, and his accessibility, boyish good looks and ideological orientation against India propelled his image. This type of ideological indoctrination works on multiple levels; substituting Kalashnikovs with clicks means gaining demographic strength within the state on mediums where India has very little or next to no legal jurisdiction. This is aided by the fact that according to census data, 63 per cent of the region's male residents are under the age of thirty and 70 per cent of them are under the age of thirty-five, many of whom are without jobs and with limited abilities and capabilities to look for work beyond the state.[3]

'Young Kashmiri minds have gone out of control,' A.S. Dulat, former chief of India's external spy agency Research and Analysis Wing (RAW) said in 2017. 'Yes, the situation is turning worse. Is it worse than in 1990? My answer is yes and no. It is worse in terms of atmospherics. Because of alienation and the anger of youth, young Kashmiri minds have gone out of control.'[4] Dulat's prognosis of youth disenchantment in the Valley is not wrong, and this disenchantment has found a medium and its own voice via the internet.

The method of using this discontent to fulfill propaganda aims shares stark similarities with the Syrian theatre of war, and is probably influenced from it. For example, both ISIS and Pakistan-supported groups in Kashmir use music to instigate their audience (or, arguably, to boost morale). Despite Islamic State's interpretation of Islam not allowing music, it produced nasheeds and released them to boost the morale of its fighters through 2016 and 2017. Hymns that are fairly austere in nature and which go as far as balancing ideological and theological agendas find an audience even within the most hard-line Islam followers.

The opposite is observable in Kashmir, as much of the fault lines for the most part of the conflict in the state have been about the state itself, and against 'occupation' by both India and Pakistan, depending on whose narrative is prevailing on a given day. While someone like Fazili created front-page space for himself via the mere act of sending an e-mail, other separatist narratives have also taken to producing slick propaganda videos.

However, of course the discourse is not the same, as videos propagating 'freedom' for Kashmir are political in nature and cannot be deemed illegal or be taken down. For example, on YouTube, all you need to do is search for Raja Rapstar, a Punjabi rap musician from Lahore, Pakistan. He gained popularity for his anti-India and pro-Kashmir songs such as 'Kashmir Ki Azadi Tak (Until Kashmir's Freedom)' and 'Hidden Blood: Kashmir New Freedom Tarana (Song)' with the latter gaining close to 40,000 views. Raja's Twitter account is blocked in India; a message displayed on his account's page says it has been withheld in response to a legal demand. 'We know who makes these, and where these are made in Pakistan,' a security official in Kashmir told this author. Other videos of Raja, which are clearly more problematic than just rap songs about Kashmiri freedom, are the ones glorifying Wani.

In one of his songs, the lyrics read: 'Will take revenge for Burhan, from the forests, but there will be no verbal talks anymore, only guns will talk, that's all.'[5] Oddly, or perhaps expectedly, a Pakistani media channel interviewing Raja introduced him as 'a Pakistani enigma that has created panic within the Indian armed forces', calling his songs and videos as part of Pakistani soft power. Whether this was a Freudian slip on the anchor's part or not is of course like many things related to Kashmir, a debate existing in the grey areas. In the same interview, the channel also showed the kind of YouTube replies Raja gets, of people from Kashmir and in Pakistan, faces covered with cloth and pledging their support for the likes of Wani and applauding Raja's music celebrating people such as Wani. In general, Kashmiri law enforcement has raised the issue of Pakistan-run disinformation campaigns publicly as well, with the state police chief Dilbag Singh also adding weight to social media increasingly becoming an issue, saying that Pakistan was now using social media to radicalize Kashmiri youth.[6]

Ultimately, the strategy of using the internet in the Valley for creation of discourse was perhaps inevitable with the massive publicity (and often a hat tip by researchers to the Islamic State for their fairly intricate online propaganda strategies) received, and the variety of documents available from ISIS and others studying these documents from researchers. More than that, it was not rocket science; there was an audience waiting and all someone had to do was create content targeted towards the said audience. Curiously, one of the main challenges this ratchets up for security forces is how do you view such output—is it music, political commentary under the freedom of speech or inciting violence against the Indian state. The security establishment expectedly sees this as something detrimental to the already frail security situation.

The content uploaded by Kashmiri militants on social media has a strong following. From calls made by militants to their families just before they were killed by security forces, an attempt to construct an image of them as martyrs for the cause and young men fighting for the Kashmiris, to produced content made across-the-border in Pakistan and distributed via chat applications, predominantly WhatsApp, have proven to be successful tactics for the militants. The popularity of such online applications in the Valley is today well documented, and information, which is often fake, about atrocities committed by Indian security forces is circulated among thousands of people within minutes as technology companies themselves struggle to fight this menace.

WhatsApp, owned by Facebook, is known to have more than 200 million active users in India alone, a figure that is growing day by day. It is, specifically from an Indian context, at the centre of everything from connecting majority of Indians with those who use it legally and those who use it as a tool to not just distribute propaganda, but to organize as well. Young men, and in some cases women as well—often leaving home telling their parents and family that they are going to pursue further education or to find work—disappear leaving the local population to try and guess what happened to them. In many cases, and in recent times more often than not, these youths appear on WhatsApp donning fatigues, and carrying guns and banners, aligning themselves with the mujahideen. This is how the family finds out, and often, the security services as well.

To illustrate this further, ISIS videos from the Middle East often find themselves tagged as videos of events that have happened in Kashmir, which only helps elevate narratives that don't exist. The 'fake news' ecosystems are a global menace, and a political quagmire such as Kashmir yields itself as an ideal place for such information warfare. In one instance, a video attributed to an instance of violence in Kashmir by security forces was actually from the Middle East but circulated and tagged its origins as being from the Valley. On Facebook, the video got hundreds of likes and more than 80,000 views. People from all over the world, sympathetic towards the militants and the separatist narrative, commented on it condemning the Indian armed forces. Despite repeated attempts of flagging the video as fake, and even a news fact checking website called Alt News doing a piece on the authenticity of the video, it took well over a month for the platform to remove the content.[7] By the time this was finally removed by Facebook, it had already been circulated in a major way in Kashmir related groups on WhatsApp.

Both ISIS-produced propaganda, which is available by the terabytes online, and the import of this strategy into the Valley is a conundrum that the Indian state seems to be fairly ill-equipped against, specifically when it comes to sensitive regions such as Kashmir. There is an evident disconnect and lack of sense of urgency between the state and the centre when it comes to countering the likes of ISIS online. 'Right now, counter-messaging and countering narratives as a policy basically means to promote the achievements and schemes of the central government and Prime Minister Modi,' an official said. The fact that, as policy, understanding of counter-messaging is equated to political promotion showcases the chronic apathy in critical thinking and understanding counterterrorism in the twenty-first century within the Indian system. Security officials on the ground in Kashmir seem to have better understanding of what is at play.

Coming back to the main point about Kashmir in the context of an entity such as the Islamic State is ultimately that like anywhere else, this ideology finds its place in vacuums. Kashmir offers that political vacuum. Nonetheless, from a larger perspective, India and its Muslim population vehemently disassociating itself from the rise of the Islamic State and the ideas driving it should be the policy establishment's go-to argument for counter-narrative programmes to dissuade youths in the Valley from falling for this trope. As far as threat perceptions around the effects ISIS has had or will have in the future being borderline paranoid, the establishment's biggest shortfall has been of being monumentally poor in understanding the fast-paced change taking place in the counterterrorism ecosystem. While this is true for Kashmir, due to the nature of the conflict, Kerala is a different ball game all together.

God's Own *Khilafat*?

More than forty-five cases of pro-ISIS activities, ranging from online propaganda to travelling abroad with the intention of joining Islamic State, have been recorded in Kerala, more than any other state in India.[1] Kerala has a large diasporic community, starting from the 1950s and 1960s when Malayalis from the state started to migrate to the Middle East illegally in dhows (small boats). Fast-forward all these decades, and nearly three million of Kerala's citizens work in the Middle East, and this relationship with the region has brought the state both fortunes and political complexities. According to some, this migration for labour and the financial upticks that come with it have kept Kerala grounded, and away from troubles of communalism and so on. 'At any point in time, the Gulf countries provided jobs to nearly 10 per cent of Kerala's working population. Without the Gulf migration, high levels of unemployment and poverty would have made Kerala a hotbed of terrorism, communalism and social tensions,' Professor Irudaya Rajan was quoted as saying a few years ago, during the peak years of pro-ISIS migration to the region from the state.[2]

Kerala's northern parts, which are predominantly Muslim, have been in the news for the number of pro-ISIS activities recorded both officially as per court documents and unofficially as far as media reports go. Dozens of people, including in some cases women and children, made their way to Iraq, Syria and Afghanistan to join ISIS and during this period, many also made it back to Kerala and successfully assimilated into normal life. Kerala's regions such as the coastal areas of Kannur saw significant spikes between 2014 and 2016 in youths travelling in attempts to join the so-called Islamic State.

In April 2017, the USA dropped a GBU-43/B Massive Ordnance Air Blast (known as MOAB, or the 'Mother Of All Bombs') in the rugged and mountainous regions of Afghanistan's Nangarhar province targeting ISIS Khorasan Province (ISKP) and its fighters also caught a few Indians from Kerala. Earlier, drone strikes against ISKP in the same month had also killed some people from Kerala, according to calls received by family members to inform them of their deaths. One of the first questions that comes up here is, why Afghanistan?

Two reasons. First, ISKP and the ecosystem that people like Armar tried to develop here from Afghanistan, as discussed earlier, still existed at some level. Much of these decisions of movement were made on convenience, and whether the radicalized travellers knew others in those areas. The total number of Indians reportedly killed in the April 2017 bombing raid is thirteen, which included a doctor and school employee, along with a two-year-old child and wives who were pregnant. Many of these people from Kerala are in fact from a similar region, in and around Kannur, and adjoining northern parts of the state.

It is hard to underplay the big role the Middle East, its financial centres, job markets and by association, politics, perform in Kerala. However, as far as ISIS and its ideological marketing in the state is concerned, the fact that there is little to no data available of Indians living in the Middle East who may have been radicalized or may have joined ISIS from there itself creates a grey area.

The distinction, and perhaps the challenge as well, that Kerala creates compared to, say, Kashmir or other parts of the country is that radicalization offline may be a bigger concern than online. Abdul Rashid Abdullah is one example of a preacher who was directly radicalizing people in Kerala and pushing them to join the Islamic State in Afghanistan. Abdullah was, like in many cases that have come up around ISIS, an educated man. Abdullah, an engineer, left his private sector job and took up preaching a hardened line of Islam after the death of his firstborn. He started teaching the Quran based on these tenets, which aligned very well with Islamic State's ideological bent. Ijas Abdul Rahman, a doctor in his mid-thirties, and his younger brother, Shiyas Abdul Rahman, in his mid-twenties, grew closer and closer to the ideology of ISIS through Abdullah's teachings, and left for Afghanistan, family in tow.

Abdullah almost justified these movements from Kerala. 'Today, it is impossible to wage offensive jihad in India. First, we have to consolidate the Caliphate, and then expand its frontiers,' he told a reporter from his hideout in Afghanistan in 2017. 'We have lots of people in India, and we tell them: wait, we're coming. The Islamic State is growing far faster than you can imagine. The aim is for the whole world to be ruled by the law of Allah, so he alone is worshipped, not false gods,' he said.

And so, like some other cases, Abdullah too evoked the political dispensation in India of the nationalist pro-Hindu BJP government of Prime Minister Modi. Abdullah called the election of Modi as a blessing in disguise, highlighting the BJP's Hindu-nationalist tenor as a background to justify his own, and others' radicalization. 'This is because while, in some parts of India, Muslims face visible oppression, in many others, they really do not recognise the reality of their oppression. The hypocrite scholars misguide them. The Modi government is planning to change the constitution and once that happens, the real oppression will begin,' he said.[3]

The rise of the nationalist Hindu discourse in Indian politics has not gone unnoticed in the pro-ISIS discussions online. Right-wing Hindu organizations such as the RSS and and VHP are often discussed as examples of why an Islamic state for Muslims is necessary, to protect themselves and the religion. In 2015, when VHP's leader Ashok Singhal died from a heart attack, pro-ISIS handles on Telegram, allegedly from India, celebrated his death. 'Good news!' one user commented. These channels also discussed about creating secure and safe zones for Muslims as they expect further strengthening of the pro-Hindu environment in the country in the time to come. While these are sporadic mentions on social media platforms, these cannot be ignored as one-offs. It ultimately, as we have seen in the examples illustrated before, takes one person to be sold a story well enough for him or her to commit an act of terror against a particular community or state.

Ultimately, theologically, ISIS propagators see one of their tasks as installing monotheism, meaning there is only one religion, that of Islam, and all others are either to be wiped out or converted to Islam. This interpretation is a driving factor of radicalization, and it is specifically dangerous in countries such as those in South Asia where secularism and globalism are precariously balanced on thin floors of religions, creeds, castes and communities living with each other. This provides an ideal canvas for organizations to create a wedge in the social fabrics of states such as India, and even Sri Lanka.

According to reports, the mastermind of the Sri Lanka terror strikes also spent time in southern India. Much of the radicalization taking place in southern India, specifically in areas such as northern Kerala, has a lot to do with the historical and current ties with the Middle East itself. These ties are not superficial, but go into the ethos of Islam, specifically Sunni Islam, as it is preached, practised, observed and distributed according to the ethos of how assimilation of Indian Muslims within the Gulf has taken place over the decades.

The ties between Islam and the people of Kerala in fact predate Islam itself, with trade between the two regions via the Arabian Sea being a prominent fixture for thousands of years. This two-way trade brought the idea of Islam to northern parts of Kerala, which embraced the same over time with locals giving land for mosques for the incoming traders. This embrace of Islam by the locals of the region was contested by both Hindus and later on the colonialists, from the Portuguese to the British. All this led to the Muslims of this region to even support Mohammed Ali Jinnah's Muslim League. These historical events helped develop a general Muslim-solidarity between the Gulf and this region, which has only been integrated much more intricately with the daily life of these parts of southern India.

Two major takeaways from the above studies of India, its pro-ISIS cases, and the people who fell for the marketing of the caliphate help provide some answers not as counterterrorism methods but to understand the ecosystem that ISIS wants to tap into better.

First, the caliphate, and travelling to it to undertake the 'holy journey', as many would end up seeing it as, turned out to be mostly a rich man's game. People who were drawn towards it, such as Mosiuddin from West Bengal, were drawn towards its state structure more than anything else. Most actively wanted to, and dreamed of living in the caliphate, which meant travel, documentation and so on. This is where many backed out, while the ideology was ingrained in them, the prospect of being told to stay where they are and conduct work for Islamic State was just not attractive enough.

Second, most Indians who were radicalized or on the cusp of it, discussing the caliphate and ISIS online on social media etc., wanted to go join, or even conduct strikes domestically for ISIS, but in groups. While cases of 'lone wolf' attacks became a tactic in Europe; in India, despite efforts of people such as Armar to push individuals to commit attacks using knives, machetes and so on, little came of it. Online radicals always looked to get together, and attempt to create groups despite the chances of being caught or information leaking out to law enforcement being fairly high compared to more obscure methods of working.

Much more empirical work needs to be done on modern jihadist groups such as ISIS and historical relations between regions, and the convergence of modernity, globalization, theology and of course, technology as far as Indian states are concerned, as blanket arguments relating to radicalization only based on historical, anthropological or religious factors do not provide many answers to questions behind an act of terrorism. Terrorism has evolved, its study must follow suit.

The Future of the Islamic State and How it will Remember the World

It was back to the parched lands clustered between the Iraqi border and the Syrian desert for the residual forces still trying to hold territory in the name of Islamic State in Baghouz—a town which saw the last holdout for the 'caliphate' that altered our very foundational understandings of terrorism, and the frameworks we developed to counter the same. September 11 designed a lot of our global approach to countering terror, and international ecosystems, multilateral forums, the United Nations so on and so forth also followed Washington's lead on how to tackle this menace, which at that time, perhaps understandably, mostly was propelled by the emotion of vengeance.

Fast forward nearly two decades and this war against terror has only expanded, and has entered deeper into grey areas of political violence, crime, militancy, insurgency, and a plethora of other violent activities. The Islamic State's designs and methods were ambitious, perhaps too ambitious, which is why its fall was prophesied early into its rise itself. Recapturing territory from the Islamic State was never going to be the difficult job, the difficult job of fighting ISIS starts now.

ISIS never stood a chance against a relentless air campaign against them by the USA, Russia, and Syrian armed forces all at the same time. ISIS itself became the magnet of global and regional concerns, managing to get even the most impossible tasks in international affairs done, such as making Russia and the USA jointly fight against the same adversary. To defeat ISIS, everyone from Al Qaeda to Washington to Moscow worked in their own silos, but towards an un-designed common goal, that of defeating the so-called khilafat.

However, one of the most important aspects to understand the rise of ISIS is to begin with the absolute basics, the fact that the terror group was not a product of the Syrian civil war; it only grew because of the conflict. Despite public perception, and arguably the idealistic push for the Arab Spring to bring down autocratic governments in the larger Middle East region by a large section of the international community, the successes of ISIS come from political vacuums, failure of governance, collapse of intra-religious and intra-tribal consensus building, and lack of economic security despite the region's oil riches. Nonetheless, despite these failings, the most important aspect of ISIS to understand is that the organization was smart, efficient, capable and more disruptive than any of its peers. In fact, a terror group that makes even the likes of Al Qaeda momentarily insecure is worthy of global scrutiny and attention.

As mentioned during the start of this book, ISIS was an insurgency first, and a proto-state second. Its proto-state version however changed our thinking of counterterrorism forever, throwing out the traditional ways of countering such groups based on human intelligence, military power and socio-economic engineering based on short-term gains. What ISIS has popularized is two different approaches, one based around the Middle East and radical Islamist thinking, not just keeping away from Western values but most moderate Islamic values as well. This is not a new way of propagating Islam for such groups; the global success of ISIS did not lie so much so in the theology itself, but on two interlinked factors.

First, land. Territory was the biggest selling point for the Islamic State; its pitch to those interested was that finally a pure land for Muslims governed by sharia law was there. The proto-state was backed by proof of control, which helped in attracting foreign fighters to come and develop the state's ecosystem. ISIS even advertized high-salaried jobs, for example working at oil refineries and wells, which they took over. This caliphate was the main marketable point to ISIS weaponizing the internet, which became the second major factor. Many analysts and researchers however contest the importance of the group's online activities and the importance given to the same in explaining its rise and how an insurgency ballooned into territorial capture larger than most countries in Europe. The fact that ISIS still dispenses online propaganda, claims attacks across the board and increasingly in more countries than ever before shows that even if the khilafat is not there anymore, the idea, and perhaps even more importantly, the brand is.

While the flow of foreign fighters may have stopped, the collapse of the Islamic State has raised more long-term problems for policymakers on how to make sure resurgence is avoided. The general perception for counterterrorism in the Middle East has mostly been via the Western microscope, which have been tremendous failures for decades on end. 'Problem with US foreign policy is that it does not have a plan beyond a six-month time frame,' a former US Air Force fighter pilot who conducted bombing runs in the region once said.

Today, there are hundreds, if not thousands, of ISIS fighters that are unaccounted for, or those who have melted away into obscurity of refugee camps and general towns and villages of both Iraq and Syria. These people may be former citizens of the caliphate, but their commitments to ISIS and its ideologies would more often than not remain strong. That means a situation has come forth where the revival of cities and towns in both the countries so affected by ISIS would also include ISIS fighters themselves, and there is no way of knowing whether they have now decided not to commit themselves towards the caliphate or they are just waiting for the opportune time to strike once again, with the 'black flag' in tow.

Keeping Iraq and Syria as they were, with the borders we know them for, is now the challenge on everyone's hands. The 'defeat' of the Islamic State is not the defeat of ISIS. How do you defeat an idea? This remains the conundrum facing everyone. The group managed to attract the educated, the professional and the trained, so the argument of radicalization of people due to their economic or societal destitution became invalid. The power and imagery of the fable sold by the Islamic State, and the piousness of the land and the religious spoils it offered leading with strong positions against non-Muslims, Westernization and other such marketable aspects promoted by the group are today etched into permanent records via the internet. This is perhaps the first time when ideology has been nestled into the safety of the binary language giving it a perpetual home, and anyone can access it whenever required.

The immediate threat from ISIS is not on the battlefield anymore, but in civilian spaces. The SDF along with the few international aid organizations working on the ground have been left with the job of taking care of the land and people in a post-ISIS region, capacity that the Kurds-led group does not have. With hundreds of people living in makeshift camps, and many ISIS fighters being held in makeshift prisons, in close proximity with each other, there is complete confusion on how to handle these camps, who will pay for them and what to do with the ISIS fighters. In fact, the celebrations of an ISIS defeat at this rate could be short-lived, as the Kurds, who first took on the weight of actually defeating ISIS and now are having to host the stateless citizens of the caliphate may have no choice but to slowly release these radicalized people back into society. Most ISIS fighters in captivity would still be what they set out to be, those who believed in the caliphate and would still like to see it make a return. And considering the political landscape in both Syria and Iraq, many would also like to think that resurgence is fully plausible.

In mid-April, an activist group working in Syria said that ISIS in the central parts of the country killed more than sixty fighters supporting the Syrian government.[1] While casualties were significant in number, this was not a one-off incident. ISIS has been active on both fronts despite their supposed defeat, and while their hierarchy has largely kept silent or is under complete hiding away from using communication tools and so on, the pro-ISIS narratives still maintain high visibility across the board.

Currently, the central Syrian region is acting as an excellent example of how not to approach the end of a terror group to make sure it does not have the intent or capabilities to restart in the near future. The challenges to defeating ISIS, fortunately or unfortunately, largely lie in Washington D.C. at the moment. Whether the world likes it or not, the de facto police of the world to its detractors, of whom there are plenty specifically in this region, US military deployed against ISIS is absolutely critical to manage the fallout of the caliphate, and to provide financial and military backup to the SDF which is the only organization on the ground currently looking to work with Western powers against ISIS.

However, this partnership is at a perilous stage itself as of December 2018. President Trump's declaration of victory against ISIS was a precursor for a troops withdrawal. On 20 December 2018, Trump tweeted: 'Getting out of Syria was no surprise. I've been campaigning on it for years, and six months ago, when I very publicly wanted to do it, I agreed to stay longer. Russia, Iran, Syria & others are the local enemy of ISIS. We were doing there work. Time to come home & rebuild. #MAGA.'[2] This abrupt withdrawal expectedly caused a flurry of concern at the Pentagon and US State Department, as both organizations, staffed with experts who have worked on the region for decades, rushed to control the damage such an abrupt move would cause. There are also indications that these decisions by the Trump administration were only found out most via his tweets, and not direct consultations.

One of the first casualties of this abrupt end to the US campaign against ISIS was Brett McGurk, the US special envoy for the global coalition to defeat ISIS. 'The recent decision by the President came as a shock and was a complete reversal of policy. It left our coalition partners confused and our fighting partners bewildered with no plan in place or even considered thought as to consequences,' McGurk said in an email he sent to his staff before resigning from his post.

McGurk and others working with partners on the Syrian front had painstakingly developed an ecosystem which would be capable and able to fight off both ISIS, and a resurgent ISIS in the future if the situation arises. The recalibration of the US anti-ISIS strategy by Trump significantly shortchanged this, by bringing down the number of US troops deployed to assist the likes of SDF to around 400, with half deployed around northeastern Syria and the other half in Al Tanf, a US military base on the Syria–Iraq border in the Homs governorate. Considering the scale of the conflict, and the fact that at a point of time Islamic State territorially was just about the same size as the UK, a residual force of 400 odd troops to back the SDF is the writing on the wall of a failed long-term policy of ensuring sustained stability.

However, a mere 400 troops expected to help maintain the sanctity of a sectarian fraught war zone is about the same as attempting to apply Band-Aid on a wound that requires reconstruction surgery. Why? Because ISIS has already proven to a certain degree that it is fairly proactive in conducting operations, not just in Syria and Iraq, but globally, and increasingly, in more countries.

In mid-April, ISIS claimed an attack in the Democratic Republic of the Congo, a vast country in the centre of the African continent, declaring it the 'Central African Province' of a caliphate, which, as far as geography goes, does not exist anymore. The claim came after a gun battle between local soldiers and unidentified armed gunmen near the town of Beni. Between April 10–16, ISIS claimed attacks in ten countries, excluding Syria and Iraq, ranging from Pakistan and Russia to Afghanistan and Egypt. These went mostly under the radar as far as international Western media goes (even elsewhere, other than the media of the countries concerned) but they happened, and this uptick coincides with the increasing number of ISIS guerrilla attacks in Syria and Iraq as well.

In the coming time, contrary to popular beliefs held not just by certain Western analysts and governments but Indian analysts as well, just because a US declaration pronounces the end of the Islamic State and Russian bombings of the same, which were at their peak in 2017, does not mean the organization has taken the defeat in its stride and retired into history.

If anything, the post-geography Islamic State is perhaps even more dangerous than the one that ruled over land, people, and resources. Controlling territory meant that there were set targets to attack against the terror group. While they flew the black flag over government buildings across Syria, and took over administrative work, set up ecosystems of policing and so forth, these structures that ISIS captured became easy targets for drone strikes and other means of air power.

Islamic State, as a state, was a driving force for recruitment. Between 2014 and 2015, people's movements in and out of Syria and to a certain extent, Iraq, were fairly lucid. At some level, it is worth accepting that if most analysts and those fighting ISIS directly knew that the proto-state will fall as fast as it rose, so did Islamic State itself. The inflow of foreign fighters from across the world was a globally covered event, however the outflow, after the collapse of the proto-state was mired in confusion with the whereabouts of thousands of ISIS fighters remaining unknown. From fighting in Syria to returning to states such as France, Britain and so on, melting back into life as if nothing had happened and often succeeding in doing so.

Today, Islamic State stands tall as a brand, a popular T-shirt that appeals to many of the youth, and one that many still would like to try on for size. The example of DR Congo is an example that personifies this strategy, as security establishments tighten the noose around pro-ISIS activities in Europe, the group's affiliates in other regions such as Southeast Asia, the African Sahel, the ISKP, Libya and so on continue to fester. The weakening of its hold on Syria means it may look to bolster its affiliates even more. Conducting attacks in Africa, other parts of the Middle East, Afghanistan and new targets such as Sri Lanka helps it build a narrative that suggests that its global reach is ever expanding despite losses in the Middle East.

The attacks in Sri Lanka will give a new lease of life to brand ISIS. The fact that their 'fighters' conducted one of the largest ever terror attack under their brand umbrella gives them immense global mileage, an aspect of their strategy which is very important to them. How to get on the front-pages of global newspapers and prime time of international news networks has been the group's modus operandi since the beginning. With Sri Lanka, ISIS achieved exactly that. It got that one big attack under its belt which was required to regain some of its lost sheen, and to signal that this is not the end of it, and more may be in the offing.

After Bangladesh in 2016, and Sri Lanka in 2019, South Asia needs to revisit its individualistic approach to counterterrorism. Transnational jihadist groups such as ISIS and Al Qaeda have got largely a free pass from both governmental approaches to counterterrorism and regional apathy. While the term 'South Asia' appears in political and geopolitical discourse as some sort of entity with unity at the core of it all, the realities are starkly different. In the coming years, the threat of terrorism will remain one step ahead of the current countering measures in place unless critical understanding is sought of how groups such as ISIS have evolved the act of committing terror. The way we gather intelligence, act upon the said intelligence and even how we identify threats has to go through a metamorphosis.

While for India, Pakistan's sponsorship of cross-border terror remains the biggest security and counterterrorism challenge, it must also not lose sight of the fact that while Pakistan-based terror groups may be trying to infiltrate the Line of Control in Jammu and Kashmir or the international border in Punjab, others such as ISIS have created direct access using the power of modern communication tools, the internet, and so on to get access to our living rooms. The questions in counterterrorism now being asked are how 'social' is social media, or how to spot radicalization and radicals living amongst us in the online sphere. How to equip our law enforcement to spot those propagating violence and extremist ideologies while sitting at a day job in the country's IT capital. And even how much an effect these organizations are having, successfully, to change our pluralist, democratic and globalist architectures of society and forcing them to shift towards populist, authoritarian and ones organized around fearmongering under the guise of national security and fear of violence from the 'others'.

These changes in the wake of the Islamic State are visible in Europe, where right-wing anti-migration politics has taken on a new life; in India, where a general anti-Muslim sentiment is seen increasingly visible in society; in Sri Lanka, where after the attacks, the minority Muslims would fear repercussions in an already fragile ethnic ecosystem and so on.

Ultimately, fighting ISIS today is not a military strategy any more. It is about fighting an idea, which is the most difficult kind of battle to win, where bullets, jets, tanks and so on fall short of achieving the aim. It is about fighting a thought, a presence that has fighters but no geography, a motivation and a battle of narratives. We have seen across examples, from Afghanistan to Syria and now Sri Lanka, that what ISIS propagates cannot be destroyed militarily, but has to be countered by society as an inclusive concept itself. Communal tensions, divisive politics, religious whataboutery to justify violence, any violence, and so on, play into the hands of organizations such as the Islamic State, which thrive in societal discord.

The Islamic State is no more, but ISIS has shown resilience. Despite the narratives that it has been defeated, the question that needs to be asked is what 'defeat' means. In his video appearance, Baghdadi has congratulated ISIS fighters for their resilience, the media operators for spreading the propaganda ever so efficiently, and new groups who pledged allegiance to him from places such as Burkina Faso and Mali in Africa. He has thrown his weight behind ISIS provinces beyond Syria and said that he expects more attacks on the West by his fighters.

ISIS may be defeated geographically, but as an idea it persists. This persistence will have no easy solutions, and the world has a long battle against an idea in front of it.

Acknowledgements

This book is the result of work predominantly conducted at the Observer Research Foundation, and is firstly, a testament to my colleagues, friends and mentors who backed my research over the past two years. Secondly, and equally as importantly, this work in its published form is also an ode to journalists across the world covering conflict zones, and bringing us reports from the frontlines. Without their tireless and selfless efforts, in many cases losing their lives in the process, researchers like us would not have much of the information on which works such as this document could be accomplished.

The author would also like to thank Prof. Harsh V. Pant, Dr Samir Saran, Dr Howard Barrell, Vidisha Mishra, Annika Taneja and many others for their contribution, time, guidance, understanding and efforts in making this possible.

Notes

Introduction

1. 'Sri Lanka attacks: Who are National Thowheed Jamath?' BBC, 28 April 2019, https://www.bbc.com/news/world-asia-48012694#.
2. Dharisha Bastians, 'Police arrest Thawheed Jamath Secretary as hate-speech, religious tensions simmer again', *Daily FT*, 17 November 2016, http://www.ft.lk/article/580594/Police-arrest-Thawheed-Jamath-Secretary-as-hate-speech--religious-tensions-simmer-again.
3. 'ISIS Chiel Refers To Sri Lanka In First Video In Five Years', NDTV, 30 April 2019, https://www.ndtv.com/world-news/isis-chief-abu-bakr-al-baghdadi-appears-for-first-time-in-5-years-in-propaganda-video-2030478.

End of the Beginning

1. Statement by India's External Affairs Minister Salman Khurshid at the Geneva-II conclave, delivered on 22 January 2014 in Switzerland, https://mea.gov.in/Speeches-Statements.htm?dtl/

22765/External+Affairs+Ministers+Statement+at+the+International+Conference+on+Syria+GenevaII.

The Origins

1. Colin Powell's speech at the UNSC on 5 February 2003, https://www.theguardian.com/world/2003/feb/05/iraq.usa.
2. Robert F. Worth, 'Blast Destroys Shrine in Iraq, Setting Off Sectarian Fury', *New York Times*, 22 February 2006 https://www.nytimes.com/2006/02/22/international/middleeast/blast-destroys-shrine-in-iraq-setting-off-sectarian.html

Welcome to Mosul

1. Charlie Winter, 'How ISIS Survives the Fall of Mosul', *Atlantic*, 3 July 2017, https://www.theatlantic.com/international/archive/2017/07/mosul-isis-propaganda/532533/.

History As Crisis

1. Refer https://jihadology.net/2014/06/29/al-%E1%B8%A5ayat-media-center-presents-a-new-video-message-from-the-islamic-state-of-iraq-and-al-sham-the-end-of-sykes-picot/.
2. Patrick Cockburn, 'Is it the end of Sykes-Picot?: The Syrian War Spills Over', *London Review of Books* 35, no. 11 (6 June 2013), pp. 3–5, https://www.lrb.co.uk/v35/n11/patrick-cockburn/is-it-the-end-of-sykes-picot.

The Arab Spring

1. Remarks by President Obama on Egypt, White House, 11 February 2011, https://obamawhitehouse.archives.gov/the-press-office/2011/02/11/remarks-president-egypt.

2. Zeynep Tufekci, *Twitter and Tear Gas: The Power and Fragility of Networked Protest* (New Haven: Yale University Press, 2017), p. 11.

The Narratives

1. Transcript of AP's interview with President Trump, 17 October 2018, https://apnews.com/ce719c7d6664400cb6b720ba84af2bc2
2. Remarks by the President at the United States Military Academy Commencement Ceremony, White House, 28 May 2014, https://obamawhitehouse.archives.gov/the-press-office/2014/05/28/remarks-president-united-states-military-academy-commencement-ceremony.

ISIS and South Asia: A Smorgasbord of Threats and Fear

1. India–GCC Relations, Ministry of External Affairs, http://www.mea.gov.in/Portal/ForeignRelation/gulf-cooperation-council-april-2012.pdf
2. Migration and Remittances Data, World Bank, 16 November 2017, http://www.worldbank.org/en/topic/migrationremittancesdiasporaissues/brief/migration-remittances-data.
3. Shreehari Paliath, 'India Remains World's Top Recipient of Remittances From Its Diaspora', BloombergQuint, 22 June 2018, https://www.bloombergquint.com/global-economics/india-remains-worlds-top-recipient-of-remittances-from-its-diaspora.
4. 'India not immune to ISIS threat, says UAE', *Economic Times*, 13 July 2018, https://economictimes.indiatimes.com/news/defence/india-not-immune-to-isis-threat-says-uae/articleshow/50902099.cms?from=mdr
5. 'Indian ISIS sympathiser deported from Saudi Arabia, arrested by NIA', *Hindustan Times*, 6 April 2017, https://www.hindustantimes.

com/india-news/indian-isis-sympathiser-deported-from-saudi-arabia-arrested-by-nia/story-iyy54C5X10xijd1vtr5T8M.html.

6. Patrick Cockburn, 'Mosul victory marks "collapse" of ISIS, says Iraqi Prime Minister', *Independent*, 10 July 2017, http://www.independent.co.uk/News/world/isis-mosul-defeat-iraq-victory-collapse-is-islamic-state-says-pm-haider-al-abadi-daesh-a7834431.html.
7. 'India Has Offered Military Assistance to Iraq in Fight Against ISIS: Iraqi Ambassador', *Wire*, 19 July 2017, https://thewire.in/diplomacy/india-offered-military-assistance-iraq-fight-isis-iraqi-ambassador.
8. For instance, while speaking on a panel titled 'The Road to 2030: Challenges, Partnerships and Predictions' during the Raisina Dialogue in January 2019, https://www.youtube.com/watch?v=kmUI_owJpL8.
9. Kabir Taneja, 'What's Behind Ties Between Assad and India?' *War on the Rocks*, 4 April 2016, https://warontherocks.com/2016/04/whats-behind-ties-between-assad-and-india/.
10. Response to a query on situation in Syria, Ministry of External Affairs, 3 September 2013, https://mea.gov.in/media-briefings.htm?dtl/22150/Response+to+a+query+on+situation+in+Syria.
11. Stanly Johny, 'Our support for Palestine remains steadfast, says Pranab', *The Hindu*, https://www.thehindu.com/news/national/president-pranab-mukherjees-sixday-trination-tour-day-2/article7750285.ece.
12. PTI, 'India abstains from voting on UNGA resolution on Syria', *Economic Times*, 12 July 2018.
13. Alan Bloomfield, 'India and the Libyan Crisis: Flirting with the Responsibility to Protect, Retreating to the Sovereignty Norm', *Contemporary Security Policy* 36, no. 1 (2015), pp. 27–55.
14. Jason Pack, Rhiannon Smith and Karim Mezran, 'The Origins and Evolution of ISIS in Libya', Atlantic Council, 20 June 2017, https://www.atlanticcouncil.org/publications/reports/the-origins-and-evolution-of-isis-in-libya

Diminished Territory, Weakened Brand?

1. 'US-backed fighters "seize 80% of Raqqa from Islamic State"', *Guardian*, 20 September 2017, https://www.theguardian.com/world/2017/sep/20/us-backed-fighters-seize-80-per-cent-raqqa-from-islamic-state-syria.
2. SyriaLive database.
3. Ibid.
4. Kabir Taneja, *Understanding ISIS: From Conception to Operations* (New Delhi: Observer Research Foundation, 2017), http://www.orfonline.org/research/understanding-isis-from-conception-to-operations/.
5. Colin P. Clarke, 'How ISIS is transforming', *Foreign Affairs*, 25 September 2017, https://www.foreignaffairs.com/articles/middle-east/2017-09-25/how-isis-transforming?cid=int-now&pgtype=hpg®ion=br2.
6. Kareem Fahim, 'The year after ISIS: The struggles of a Sunni village in northern Iraq', *Washington Post*, 27 September 2017, https://www.washingtonpost.com/world/middle_east/the-year-after-isis-the-struggles-of-a-sunni-village-in-northern-iraq/2017/09/27/8ed3863a-76dc-11e7-8c17-533c52b2f014_story.html?tid=sm_tw_pw&utm_term=.4215d564d274&wprss=rss_world_twpstaffonly; Mustafa Habib, 'Locals In Former Extremist Areas Live In Ruins, Cope With Lawless Militias', *Niqash*, http://www.niqash.org/en/articles/security/5742/Locals-In-Former-Extremist-Areas-Live-In-Ruins-Cope-With-Lawless-Militias.htm.
7. Tim Lister, Jim Sciutto, Ghazi Balkiz and Michael Callahan, 'ISIS leader seemingly breaks 11-month silence in audio recording', CNN, 30 September 2017, http://edition.cnn.com/2017/09/28/politics/isis-baghdadi-audio-recording/index.html.
8. R. Green, 'Dispute Over Takfir Rocks Islamic State', MEMRI, 4 August 2017, https://www.memri.org/reports/dispute-over-takfir-rocks-islamic-state.

9. Copy of full speech accessed by the author.
10. Audrey Morallo, 'Marawi siege "most serious terror event" in Southeast Asia in past 15 years', *PhilStar.com*, 25 August 2017, http://www.philstar.com/headlines/2017/08/25/1732611/marawi-siege-most-serious-terror-event-southeast-asia-past-15-years.
11. 'To fight ISIS, India grants Rs 3.2 crore aid to Philippines', Times Now, 12 July 2017, http://www.timesnownews.com/india/article/to-fight-isis-india-grants-rs-3-crore-aid-to-philippines/65695.
12. *Tracking ISIS' influence in India: Studying a dynamic global war via New Delhi*, Observer Research Foundation, http://trackingisis.orfonline.org/.
13. Aravind Gowda, 'Not merely a sympathizer, Mehdi Masroor Biswas represented ISIS: Bengaluru police', *India Today*, 3 June 2015, http://indiatoday.intoday.in/story/isis-mehdi-masroor-biswas-bengaluru-police-abu-bakr-al-bhagdadi-islamic-caliphate/1/442022.html.
14. Paritosh Bansal and Serajul Quadir, 'New Evidence Reveals Deep ISIS Involvement In Bangladesh Massacre', *Wire*, 1 December 2016, https://thewire.in/83685/new-evidence-isis-involvement-bangladesh/.
15. '"This Will Repeat, Repeat, Repeat," Says ISIS About Dhaka Cafe Attack', *NDTV*, 6 July 2016, https://www.ndtv.com/world-news/isis-says-dhaka-cafe-slaughter-a-glimpse-of-whats-coming-1428546.
16. This information is a corroboration of information from charge sheets accessed by the author, unavailable for public discourse at the time of writing.
17. The Bangladeshi military official and his family member's story was told to the author during talks with officials in a visit to Dhaka.
18. Borhan Osman, 'The Islamic State in "Khorasan": How it began and where it stands now in Nangarhar', Afghanistan Analysts Network, 27 July 2016, https://www.afghanistan-analysts.org/

the-islamic-state-in-khorasan-how-it-began-and-where-it-stands-now-in-nangarhar/.

19. 'French ISIS fighters move to Afghanistan after facing defeat in Syria', Khaama Press, 10 December 2017, https://www.khaama.com/french-isis-fighters-move-to-afghanistan-after-facing-defeat-in-syria-04015.
20. Richard Barrett, *Beyond the Caliphate: Foreign Fighters and the Threat of Returnees* (New York: The Soufan Center, October 2017), p. 13, https://thesoufancenter.org/wp-content/uploads/2017/11/Beyond-the-Caliphate-Foreign-Fighters-and-the-Threat-of-Returnees-TSC-Report-October-2017-v3.pdf.
21. Charlie Winter and Haroro J. Ingram, 'Why ISIS Is So Good At Branding Its Failures As Successes', *Atlantic*, 19 September 2017, https://www.theatlantic.com/international/archive/2017/09/isis-propaganda/540240/.
22. 'Amaq reports first attack in Kashmir valley with killing of police officer in Srinagar', *SITE Intelligence*, 18 November 2017, https://ent.siteintelgroup.com/Statements/amaq-reports-1st-is-attack-in-kashmir-valley-with-killing-of-police-officer-in-srinagar.html;

    Peerzada Ashiq, 'Probe on into IS claim on Srinagar attack', *The Hindu*, 19 November 2017, https://www.thehindu.com/news/national/islamic-states-magazine-claims-responsibility-for-srinagar-attack/article20555507.ece.
23. Winter and Ingram, 'Why ISIS Is So Good At Branding Its Failures As Successes'.
24. Paul Staniland, 'Whither ISIS? Insights from Insurgent Responses to Decline', *Washington Quarterly 40,* no. 3 (2017), pp. 29–43.
25. Ibid.
26. Ibid.
27. Charles Lister, 'Al-Qaeda Versus ISIS: Competing Jihadist Brands in the Middle East' (Washington D.C., Middle East Institute, 2017), p. 4, https://www.mei.edu/sites/default/files/publications/PP3_Lister_CTQaeda_0.pdf.

28. *Quarterly Report to the United States Congress* (Arlington: SIGAR, October 30 2017), https://www.sigar.mil/pdf/quarterlyreports/2017-10-30qr.pdf.
29. *Neta C. Crawford, United States Budgetary Costs of the Post 9/11 Wars Through FY2019: $5.9 Trillion Spent and Obligated* (Providence: Watson Institute, November 2018), https://watson.brown.edu/costsofwar/files/cow/imce/papers/2018/Crawford_Costs%20of%20War%20Estimates%20Through%20FY2019%20.pdf.
30. Jon Boone, 'Pakistan launches crackdown as Isis shrine attack toll rises to 88', *Guardian,* 17 February 2017, https://www.theguardian.com/world/2017/feb/16/thirty-killed-100-injured-isis-bomb-sufi-shrine-pakistan-sindh.
31. Salman Masood, 'ISIS Claims Suicide Bombing That Killed at Least 15 in Pakistan', *New York Times*, 13 August 2017, https://www.nytimes.com/2017/08/13/world/asia/pakistan-suicide-bomber-motorbike.html.
32. This excerpt is from a charge sheet accessed by the author. Further details were unavailable for public disclosure at the time of writing.

The Post-ISIS Era

1. Erika Solomon and Ahmad Mhidi, 'ISIS finds escape routes for the profits of war', *Financial Times*, 23 August 2017, https://www.ft.com/content/b2f616d4-8656-11e7-8bb1-5ba57d47eff7.
2. Jason Burke, 'The Age of Selfie Jihad: How Evolving Media Technology Is Changing Terrorism', *CTC Sentinel 9*, no. 11 (November/December 2016), https://ctc.usma.edu/posts/the-age-of-selfie-jihad-how-evolving-media-technology-is-changing-terrorism.

The Attempts to Create ISIS in India

1. Raed Asad Ahmed, 'Kurdish Judge Who Ordered Saddam Hanged is Alive and Well', Rudaw, 26 June 2014, http://www.rudaw.net/english/kurdistan/260620143.

2. *Tracing the Supply of Components Used in Islamic State IEDs* (London: Conflict Armament Research, February 2016), http://www.conflictarm.com/wp-content/uploads/2016/02/Tracing_The_Supply_of_Components_Used_in_Islamic_State_IEDs.pdf.

'The ISIS Pool'

1. Sagnik Chowdhury, 'Mehdi Masroor Biswas: Terror's propaganda tweets via Gulf, India', *Indian Express*, 20 November 2015, https://indianexpress.com/article/india/india-news-india/mehdi-masroor-biswas-terrors-propaganda-tweets-via-gulf-india/.
2. Hassan Hassan, 'The Unmasking of an Islamic State Twitter Troll', *Foreign Policy*, 17 December 2014, https://foreignpolicy.com/2014/12/17/the-unmasking-of-an-islamic-state-twitter-troll-shami-witness-mehdi-mansoor-biswas/.

The Online Six Degrees of Separation

1. The issue of Rumiyah was accessed on Jihadology.net, an academic repository of Islamist jihadist propaganda and paraphernalia. This academic resource is currently banned from access by the Indian government.
2. Arunima, 'Air Hostess Who Recruited 20 Indians For ISIS on WhatsApp, Facebook Reveals Details of Gulf Money Trail', News18, 3 May 2018, https://www.news18.com/news/india/air-hostess-who-recruited-20-indians-for-isis-on-whatsapp-facebook-reveals-details-of-gulf-money-trail-1737901.html.

Schrödinger's Thirty-nine

1. Dilip Bobb, 'Muted reaction to Gulf crisis isolates India', *India Today*, 15 October 1990, https://www.indiatoday.in/magazine/diplomacy/story/19901015-muted-reaction-to-gulf-crisis-isolates-india-813116-1990-10-15.

2. External Affair Minister's Statement after meeting with families of Indians in captivity in Iraq, 22 February 2015, https://www.mea.gov.in/media-advisory.htm?dtl/24795/External+Affairs+Ministers+Statement+after+meeting+with+families+of+Indians+in+captivity+in+Iraq.
3. Alia Allana, 'The One Who Got Away', *Fountain Ink*, 31 July 2015, https://fountainink.in/reportage/the-one-who-got-away-.
4. Kabir Taneja, 'No gains: Indian special envoy exits from Erbil', *Sunday Guardian*, 17 January 2015, http://www.sunday-guardian.com/news/no-gains-indian-special-envoy-exits-from-erbil.
5. 'Iraq: ISIS Executed Hundreds of Prison Inmates', Human Rights Watch, 30 October 2014, https://www.hrw.org/news/2014/10/30/iraq-isis-executed-hundreds-prison-inmates.
6. Ibid.

From Kashmir to Kerala: ISIS and its Narratives

1. 'ISIS flags in Srinagar, MHA seels report', *Times of India*, 13 October 2014, https://timesofindia.indiatimes.com/videos/news/ISIS-flags-in-Srinagar-MHA-seeks-report/videoshow/44799121.cms.
2. Kabir Taneja, 'Islamic State merits high caution but not careless alarmism in Kashmir', *Scroll.in*, 20 October 2014, https://scroll.in/article/684087/islamic-state-merits-high-caution-but-not-careless-alarmism-in-kashmir.
3. Mir Ehsan, 'Four militants killed in Kashmir encounter inspired by Islamic State, say police', *Hindustan Times*, 22 June 2018, https://www.hindustantimes.com/india-news/gunfight-breaks-out-between-security-forces-militants-in-jammu-and-kashmir-s-anantnag/story-oCWZ8AdREp6bz4aeTQpLMM.html.
4. 'No ISIS in Kashmir, says DGP', *Northlines*, 28 February 2018, http://www.thenorthlines.com/no-isis-kashmir-says-dgp/.
5. PTI, 'No presence of Islamic State in Kashmir: MHA', *Livemint*, 27 February 2018, https://www.livemint.com/Politics/SBg4mmX5HZ5OBZQvbuhMqN/No-presence-of-Islamic-State-in-Kashmir-MHA.html.

6. 'Eisa Fazili: A Militant? Martyr? But First A Son', *ViewPoint*, 16 March 2018, https://www.viewpoint.net.in/2018/03/eisa-fazili-militant-martyr-son/ and screenshot of original Facebook post by Aamir Ahmad Amin, https://imgur.com/d9aY0uT.

'I am in the News with an ISIS Flag'

1. 'ISIS targeting foreigners in Kolkata with JMB, planning lone wolf attacks in Srinagar?' Zee News, 3 January 2017, https://zeenews.india.com/kolkata/isis-targeting-foreigners-in-kolkata-with-jmb-planning-lone-wolf-attacks-in-srinagar_1963877.html.
2. Animesh Roul, 'Jamaatul Mujahidin Bangladesh: Weakened, But Not Destroyed', *CTC Sentinel* 4, no. 11 (November 2011), https://ctc.usma.edu/jamaatul-mujahidin-bangladesh-weakened-but-not-destroyed/.

Narrating Kashmir and Terror

1. 'An interview with Burhan Wani's father', *Hindustan Times*, 9 July 2016, https://www.youtube.com/watch?v=CGi9eK-MPFo.
2. Kabir Taneja and Kriti M. Shah, 'The conflict in Jammu & Kashmir and the Convergence of Technology and Terrorism', Royal United Services Institute (RUSI), 7 August 2019 https://rusi.org/publication/other-publications/conflict-jammu-and-kashmir-and-convergence-technology-and-terrorism
3. India National Census Data 2011, http://censusindia.gov.in/2011-Common/CensusData2011.html
4. 'Situation in Kashmir never scarier, RAW's former chief', *Dawn*, 4 May 2017, https://www.dawn.com/news/1330963.
5. Raja Rapstar, Kashmir Ki Azadi Tak, YouTube, October 2018, https://www.youtube.com/watch?v=n5hqa_dXz-I
6. 'Pakistan Using Social Media To "Radicalise" Kashmiri Youths: Top Cop', NDTV, 30 January 2019, https://www.ndtv.com/india-news/pakistan-using-social-media-to-radicalise-kashmiri-youths-top-cop-1985263.

7. Pooja Chaudhuri, 'Old video from Syria viral as Indian Army's atrocities on Kashmiri women', *Alt News*, 8 February 2019, https://www.altnews.in/old-video-from-syria-viral-as-indian-armys-atrocities-on-kashmiri-women/.

God's Own *Khilafat*?

1. ISIS Tracker, Observer Research Foundation, http://trackingisis.orfonline.org/.
2. S. Sanandakumar, 'A fifty year old phenomenon explained: Malayalee migration to Gulf builds the new Kerala', *Economic Times*, 3 October 2015, https://economictimes.indiatimes.com/news/politics-and-nation/a-fifty-year-old-phenomenon-explained-malayalee-migration-to-gulf-builds-the-new-kerala/articleshow/49201357.cms.
3. Praveen Swami, 'From Afghan hideout, Kerala jihad leader calls faithful to Caliphate', *Indian Express*, 18 May 2017, https://indianexpress.com/article/india/from-afghan-hideout-kerala-jihad-leader-calls-faithful-to-caliphate-4661362/.

The Future of Islamic State and How it will Remember the World

1. 'Militants kill more than 60 pro-Syrian government forces: Activist group', *Middle East Eye*, 20 April 2019, https://www.middleeasteye.net/news/militants-kill-more-60-pro-syrian-government-forces-activist-group.
2. President Donald Trump's tweet on 20 December 2018 (the President's tweets are riddled with inaccuracies and poor grammar, the republishing of those tweets appears with the errors as tweeted by him), https://twitter.com/realDonaldTrump/status/1075718191253504001?.